Water&Salt

The Essence of Life

The Healing Power of Nature

Contents

5   Acknowledgements

6   Foreword by:
     Dr. med. Barbara Hendel,
     Peter Ferreira

| 8 | The Ocean |

Origin of Life

| 12 | The Biophysics |

The Realm of Living Energy

17   Biochemistry versus Biophysics

22   Life-Force and Energy

23   Energy and Information

32   Health and Disease from a
     Biophysical Point of View

37   Looking at Food from a
     Biophysical Point of View

| 44 | The Water |

The Pillar of Life

48   Water – An Extraordinary
     Element

56   The Movement of Water

60   The Healing Properties of Water

67   The Quality of our Water

75   The Processing of Water

80   FIJI Natural Artesian Water

| 96 | The Salt |

The White Gold of Earth

99   Water and Salt – Building Blocks
     of Life

102 The Structure of Salt

108 From White Gold To White
     Poison

116   Natural Salt Resources

126   The Healing Powers of Salt

129   Research Findings

144   The Sole

Symbiosis of Life-Force

148   The Creation of Life

155   The Healing Effects of Sole

160   The Forms

The Various Applications of Salt

163   The Sole Drinking Therapy

165   Sole Inhalation

165   Flushing Your Sinus with Sole

168   The Sole Bath

171   The Floatation Tank

174   Topical Applications of Sole

176   Sole Wraps

178   Salt Sachet Applications

178   Body Peeling

181   Sole Mud (Peloid)

183   Crystal Salt Ionizer

184   Crystal Salt Lamps

186   The Applications

Practical Examples of
Salt Applications

189   The Skin

200   Allergies

205   Colds

211   Diseases of the Locomotive
      System

217   Indigestion and Malfunctioning
      Metabolism

⟹ 218   Kidney and Bladder Problems

220   Cordiovascular Diseases

221   Nervousness, Poor Concentration, Sleeping Disorders

222   Cancer

224   Womens Health Issues

225   Diseases of the Eye

227   Heavy Metals

228   Oral Hygiene

229   Salt-Based Skin & Body Care and Wellness

236 | Appendix

236   Bibliography

238   Product Suppliers

239   Personal Dedications

240   Imprint

241   Special Note

242   Glossary

247   Index

232 | In Conclusion

Enhance your Consciousness

We give thanks to all those scientists, physicians and idealists who, through an inner calling and their idealism, are willing to walk new paths, against the odds and the resistance of the dogmas of the scientific establishment. We want to express our gratitude to the following people without whom this book, and all its information, would not have been possible:

Dr. Faridum Batmanghelidj, Doug Carlson, Dr. Enza Cicollo, Gudrun Dalla Via, Dr. Masuru Emoto, Liv von Finckenstein, Dr. Patrick Flanagan, David & Jill Gilmour, Carl Heiney, Wolfgang Heisler, Prof. Roland Höck, Dr. Wilhelm Höfer, Dr. Marianne Huber, Dr. Elisabeth Josenhans, Prof. Manfred Kage, Klaus Kaufmann, Dr. Noemi Kempe, Bodo Köhler, Ruth Kübler, Dr. Jacques De Langres, Ed & Ingrid Leach, Shoshana Leibner, Prof. John Lilly, Dr. Wolfgang Ludwig, Frank Mitchell, Prof. Fritz-Albert Popp, Heidemaria Schornsteiner, Dr. Bruce Shelton, Denise Sommerfeld, Rudolf Steiner, Heinz Steinmeyer, Vivian Vukojevich, Daniel Weinberg, and Dr. Barbara Werner. Special thanks for their open-mindedness and support goes to GeoGlobe – Development & Marketing Corporation, represented by Augustin Schöpf and Horst Thöni. We would also like to give thanks to all those physicians and therapists who walk new paths in service to humanity, as well as to all the journalists having the courage and wisdom to make this kind of information available to the public at large.

From the first day that this book was introduced in Germany two years ago, it was an immediate bestseller. Millions of people have changed their lives in respect to water and salt with the profound scientific information presented herein in an easy-to-read format that everyone is able to understand. We are happy to now make our English speaking readers acquainted with the subjects of Water & Salt so that they too may find better understanding and respect for these most essential elements. We also hope that thousands of doctors, scientists, alternative practitioners and therapists will embrace this natural knowledge to help mankind in a natural way.

Why was this book written? Water & Salt actually originated from an interest generated by those who attended, with increasing interest, the seminars where the scientific research and holistic understanding regarding the two natural elements of water and salt, was presented. Many attendees realized the positive health implications of these research findings while gaining a more positive outlook to their personal lives. The fact about these two most natural and simple subjects of water & salt made a lot of sense to most of the people, but many questions still remained unanswered. It appeared that this ancient knowledge regarding the laws of nature had been lying dormant in the darkness for too long. How could we take the dusty bottles of knowledge from the cellar and give them new labels and present them anew? Although the answers to the remaining questions seemed to be self-explanatory by simple logic, many people were looking for proof. So, for you, this book is meant to be a useful and practical guide. For those of you wanting even more, this book will not only give you some scientific knowledge, but can act as a catalyst for a new, healthier and independent life.

The goal of the authors is to make the life-giving properties of water and salt understandable to everyone. Nature is less complicated than we think. In fact, with orderly simplicity, nature reveals its cosmic laws. It is only up to us to recognize and understand it again. Once we comprehend the connections, an inner impulse will ignite the change.

This precious knowledge shall not be kept within a small circle of scientifically trained people. With the public's growing interest in the subject of water and salt, this book has been written in a holistically minded way for the average person. The expectations of this book will be fulfilled when the individual reader will experience an impulse for change, not only to recognize the purpose of life, but also to experience it. Our whole life is a continuously developing process towards a higher state of consciousness.

Reading this book will demystify the mysterious and provide a new outlook, one which may challenge many of the old dogmas and credos. Many will feel the urge to reevaluate their present views. But we also encourage our readers to accept this knowledge with a critical eye. Real knowledge comes only from your own experience. Listen to your inner voice and then make your own practical experiences. Be suspicious when things are changed from their original state. Our aim is not only to inform, but also to inspire and motivate our readers to recognize creation not only on the outside but to experience it on the inside. Real Life must be experienced! Experience real life!

We wish you much success along your path to your new way of life!

Peter Ferreira and Dr. med. Barbara Hendel, August 2003

The

Ocean

Origin of Life

Millions of years ago, Earth was a watery planet. Totally enveloped in a salty, primal ocean, the land we walk upon today appeared over countless millennia as the subsiding seas were slowly evaporated by the energy of the sun. Still today, over seventy percent of the Earth is covered in water, which is why our planet is also referred to as the "blue planet." Her mesmerizing blue color and awe-striking beauty has fascinated astronauts since man first entered space.

70% of our Earth, the "Blue Planet", is covered with salt water

Sole (so-lay): The Foundation for the Creation of Life

Life comes from the ocean. The water of the ocean – a natural *sole* (water and salt solution) – contains the essential energy for the creation of life. All life forms on this planet have emerged from the ocean. We can observe this process in the growth of a fetus in the womb. Beginning from the day of conception, the embryo passes through all developmental stages of evolution. After 5 weeks it develops fish-like gills that slowly recede. Two hundred and fifty million years (250,000,000) of evolution are performed in this period – from one single cell to a human being with consciousness. Where does this new life start? In the womb, in the amniotic fluid, in a 98.6°F, one percent water and salt solution (one part salt, 100 parts water) – the *sole*. This natural salt solution, called *sole*, is from the origin of the word, directly connected to the word "soul". What we call *sole* for our

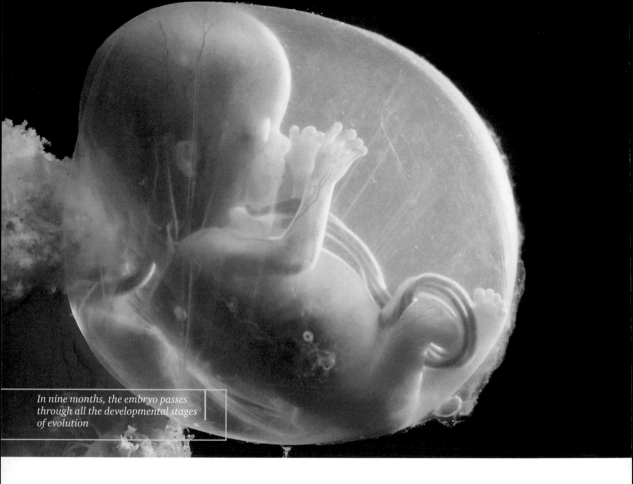

In nine months, the embryo passes through all the developmental stages of evolution

salt solution (solution-two in one-no more polarity), was believed by the ancient Celts to represents our soul, as the soul originated, in their belief, from the ocean where we are all born from the same fluids, arising from the same "soul."

On the Self Healing Power of the Body

Our body is always striving to maintain its natural balance

Our body in its wholeness is an ingenious creation of nature. It has been given all mechanisms to not only sustain its life but also to create new life. Every healthy person has innate regulatory mechanisms and self-healing powers, which ensure or reestablish the natural balance of the bodily functions, the homeostasis. It is not the doctor that heals us, nor the medication, but our own

innate regulatory mechanisms. Our body is able to fully regenerate itself. Therefore, it is advised to use great discernment
before labeling any disease as "incurable." If doctors come to
the conclusion that a disease is incurable, they would be more
accurate in saying that with their knowledge and experience,
they are not able to offer any further help. The word "incurable"
conveys fear, which stifles and weakens our body's innate
defense mechanisms.

More Than Just Matter

If we enable our body, with the help of water and salt, to regulate itself, the body is able to regenerate itself and conquer
every disease. We can reestablish the primal order in our body
with the help of these original elements. The qualities of water
and salt do not, by any means, originate in their material
makeup or purity alone. We are not only speaking of the chemical composition of these two elements, but rather about their
holistic qualities. The science of biophysics plays a key role
within this perspective. On the basis of these findings, you will
rediscover water and salt and appreciate the unique and all-
encompassing possibilities of maintaining health and preventing
many ailments. The science of biophysics offers you a perspective
of the world that will raise your consciousness and offer you a
holistic approach to life.

The chemical point of view alone falls short: water and salt are much more than mere chemical formulas

Even modern science no longer refers to water as simply H_2O
and to salt as NaCl (sodium chloride). The chemical and biochemical attributes of water and salt arise from a series of far
reaching biophysical and energetic interactions. It is the goal of
this book to show you and help you to understand the holistic
abilities of water and salt; and when you understand these
interactions, you will be inspired to change your ways. And,
you will be abundantly rewarded with an expansion in consciousness that comes with this understanding.

The

Biophysics

The Realm of Living Energy

To understand the secrets of water and salt, we want to invite you to take an excursion into the fascinating world of biophysics. In contrast to chemistry and mechanical physics, which focus primarily on the conditions and appearances of "dead" matter, biophysics studies the entire biological organism. Biophysical science is devoted to the study of vital living matter (Greek: bios = life), starting from the mineral and plant kingdom up to and including animals and humans. This science only recently emerged from the scientific fringes.

Distinguishing Biophysics from Biochemistry

If we only study matter, as in physics, we only understand matter. However, there are things we cannot explain materially. This is exactly the area that biophysics is devoted to. Through its one-sided, mechanical world view, classical natural science has distanced itself far from its original goal – to derive knowledge from nature. Today, only that which can be scientifically proven is accepted in science. However, most of the research areas within the natural sciences are not natural sciences. Even physics calls upon mechanics in its discoveries, and mechanics, for that matter, calls upon the wheel, and the wheel upon the circle. This circle symbolizes the repeatability of an experiment. Only when the same experiment arrives at the same conclusions over and over again, can we call the outcome scientifically proven, and it can then find its way into our books. However, we must

If matter is all that we search for, matter is all that we will find

A spiraling nebula – even in the depth of the cosmos we find the life-ruling pattern of the spiral

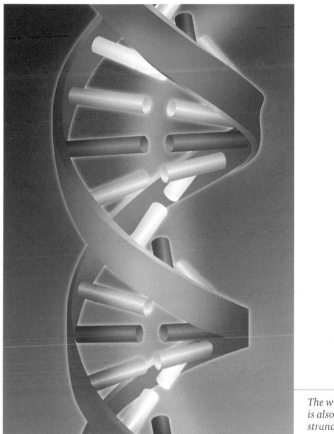

The winding spiral is also found in strands of DNA

have forgotten that there are no such circles in nature. What we find in nature is the spiral. Wherever we look in nature, we find the spiral form, be it the spiraling nebula or our spiraling DNA.

Nature knows no stagnation, only the dynamics of constant renewal

The Spiral as a Symbol of Natural Order

Although the spiral returns to its original point, this point no longer exists on the same level as it did in its beginning. Consider the four seasons. Every year we experience anew the birth and death of the natural cycles. But the vast seasonal forms of expression are unique despite their ever-repeating cycles. Each day is unique; the previous one is never the same as the present one. Therefore, nature cannot be forced into an objective, empirically based framework. Even though we, as humans, are

The seasons: repeating every year, yet never the same

subject to the same natural laws, we cannot conclude that what is true for one is also true for another. This is the reason why traditional scientific research methods, justifiably used in physics, are not appropriate for biophysics.

What Distinguishes Biophysics from Physics

Mechanical physics studies the conditions and appearances of dead matter. In contrast, biophysics studies the entire biological organism from the mineral and plant kingdom to animals and humans.

Biochemistry vs. Biophysics

Classical allopathic medicine is mostly navigated by biochemistry, the science of chemical procedures in the human body. This means that we only accept the existence of that which we

can see and touch. But if we are only looking for matter or at the material level, material or matter is all we'll find. It is known that cancer develops in the body over a number of years, without revealing itself to our hi-tech diagnostic instruments. Only after the cancer has materialized and assumed structure in the form of tumorous tissue, we can find it. However, by this time it is already the eleventh hour. It would be blessedly profound if we could measure the energetic deficit in a cancer patient with biophysical measurement methods in order to prevent the worst-case scenario.

Such methods already exist in their infancy stages and are starting to be applied. For example, we can measure energetic potential in acupuncture points through measurements in skin resistance, with the help of segmentary diagnostics and

With the help of bioenergetic measurements we will soon be able to recognize cancer in its early stages

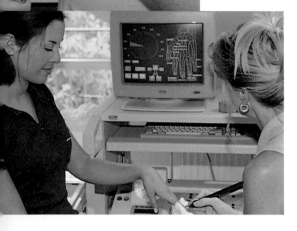

We can measure energetic potentials through electronic acupuncture, which recognizes even the slightest distortions of organs

organometry as well as electronic acupuncture, thus revealing the condition of the respective organ. However, until the medical establishment supports the biochemical standpoint or accepts biophysical phenomena, imperative research in this area cannot take place. Max Planck remarked aptly: "A new scientific understanding usually cannot be presented in a way that would convince its adversaries. Only after they pass away can the new truth be implemented through the next generation, who is accustomed to the new paradigm."

How Biochemistry Influences Lifestyle

Even health-conscious people are mostly focused on biochemical aspects by supplementing their diet with vitamins, minerals, trace elements, enzymes, amino acids and other vital elements. At the end of the day the question is, have they really given their body what it needed? And, how are we supposed to

Electro-Acupuncture by Voll (EAV)

EAV is a painless measurement method to diagnose and therapeutically alleviate dysfunctions in the body. It is based on classical Chinese acupunture. A healthy organism is energetically balanced. With the computerized EAV, even the smallest distortions of the organs can be revealed. With this full-body check-up, an early diagnosis can be made before a disease materializes. This is preventative medicine. EAV identifies the source of physical symptoms, especially those that manifest in the teeth, and recognizes energy blockages. Allergies can be tested and toxic stresses can be revealed.

nourish ourselves appropiately in times of depleted soils, when our fresh produce allegedly no longer includes the essential elements for maintaining sound health? In desperation, many of us reach for supplements in order to compensate for these deficits. If our body needs calcium, which is not available in sufficient quantities from the food we eat, a calcium pill should do the trick. This seems plausible from a biochemical point of view.

Consuming pills for nutrition instead of natural foods is a poor trade-off

Quality Versus Quantity

Biophysically, we must ask the question as to whether or not our bodies can absorb this isolated, inorganic calcium in the form of a supplement. You may ingest fifty pounds of calcium pills, yet your cells would still have less calcium than if you would have eaten only one carrot. The calcium supplement is partially absorbed by the body and can be traced in the blood. However, due to the supplement's gross, inorganic, material form, the cells cannot absorb it. Whatever the cells do not absorb cannot be metabolized and consequently, is useless to the body. At this point you may ask why this simple fact is not widely known. One of the answers might be that far more profits can be made by selling supplements than by selling carrots. In the U.S. alone, profits from food supplements have reached a volume of over $16 billion a year. Plus billions of dollars more of revenue are made from selling of items categorized as general nutrition products, many of which have nothing to do with real nutrition.

The body's cells can only absorb minerals in their organic or ionalcolloidal form

The important biophysical aspects are given little attention in regards to health questions. In biophysics it is exclusively the quality that counts, not the quantity. Through the ever-greater expansion of a material-chemical viewpoint of life, like isolating vitamins from fruit, humanity has isolated itself from a natural way of living. So it is not surprising that over time we have lost our understanding for this simple, natural relation.

At this point we shall come back to water and salt. Both of these elements are essential, not only for keeping us alive in a chemical sense, but most importantly for their quality, their vitality – their energetic and biological activity.

It is no mistake that water is known to be our primary source of nourishment. As you will see, salt, in its original, natural form, is equally important.

One billion energy units are required to produce one single unit of matter

How Energy Creates Matter

In 1984, Dr. Carlos Rubbia, an atomic physicist from Switzerland, received the Nobel Prize for discovering a mathematically calculable natural constant with which he could calculate the ratio of mass particles (matter) in relation to navigating energy particles. The ratio of matter to energy that forms matter is 1: 9,746 x 108. This corresponds to about 1:1,000,000,000 – which means it takes one billion energy units to create one single unit of matter in a materialized tangible form. Isn't it interesting that we, for the most part, preoccupy ourselves with only a one billionth part of reality: that which is in a material form and can be seen and touched. We fail to see the far greater amount of energy particles it took to materialize our reality. This revolutionary scientific discovery shows us clearly that every form of matter is subject to higher energetic interactions.

The Biochemical and Biophysical View of Matter

This example will illustrate the difference between biophysics and biochemistry. When we analyze a living and a freshly-deceased human body, chemically speaking we will not find any difference between them. Every biochemist will confirm that there has been no alteration in the bones or organs, even the cell structure and the molecules are the same, given that the examination takes place immediately following death. The weight remains the same and even the temperature can be more or less the same. However, one body is alive and the other is dead. The dead body will decompose and return to its fundamental components, dust of the earth. One and the same matter!

What power, we shall ask here, what kind of energy does it take to form structure from matter, from apparently lifeless material, and keep it together in order to create this living body? This is exactly what we examine and study in biophysics.

The difference between biochemistry and biophysics becomes clear in the example of a body immediately following death

---

What Distinguishes Biochemistry from Biophysics

Biochemistry examines those chemical procedures in living beings that are materially demonstrable.
Biophysics looks at the abilities of energetic interactions and reciprocities of living matter.

Life-Force and Energy

Life, like energy, cannot be destroyed; it simply transforms

Physics defines what we describe as "alive," as energy. Energy can always be transformed but can never be destroyed or cease to be. Physics can only recognize these ever-changing forms, but cannot distinguish between dead and living. Every object that we perceive as lifeless, such as a table, a glass or a stone, as any other form of matter, is a vibrating form of energy. But how exactly shall we imagine this inextinguishable activity that we call energy in physics?

Vibrating Energy, the Origin of Life

When we analyze the energy content of any form of matter, we arrive at its smallest part, the atom. Every atom has a nucleus at its core that is encircled by electrons. There is ongoing movement without any contact – nothing tangible, just pure vibrating energy. This vibrating energy creates a frequency, a so-called wavelength. Every form of matter is characterized by its specific frequency spectrum. We can only see the effect of this frequency spectrum for example, when we turn on a light or an electrical device. However, we cannot perceive the electrical current itself. And even though we cannot see, taste or touch electricity, we still accept its existence. This same materially non-perceivable electricity, this energy, flows through our body. Everyone of us has enough measurable electrical current flowing through us to light up a 100-watt light bulb. Where does this energy come from, this life-force? Where can we find this cause of life?

Every form of matter, every stone, every plant, every animal, and every human being consists of pure vibrating energy

Lightning is an especially impressive example of the power of electric energy

Energy and Information

Life is equivalent to energy. Life = Energy, Energy = Information. Energy, according to physics, is equivalent to "information", as we shall explain. Everything that exists not only exists as energy but also as a carrier of information, whether it is a human being or any form of food in its natural state of wholeness. Life is a constant exchange of energy and information. The medium/matter is less important than the information contained within.

23

Information – The Basis of Order

How can we envision or visualize this? Every form of energy has an associated form of vibration, a wavelength that is measurable as an electromagnetic frequency. Each wavelength contains its own inherent information. There is no coincidence in the cosmic order, nothing arbitrary. Every form of energy strives to manifest itself according to a precisely defined energetic blueprint. We can even find this energetic ambition anchored in the word "information." The word means to "come into form" according to a preexisting order (Latin for form = forma). So every material manifestation, every mineral, every plant, every animal, and every human being is an assembly of all the information involved: all wavelengths, energies and all the life-force that follows the impulses of a higher order.

Matter is not subject to the principle of coincidence, but to a stable, energetic blueprint

---

Revealing the Origin of Life-Energy

The classic, natural science which reveals the source of everything, can be proven mostly through mathematics. The name in itself reveals the trinity of body, mind, and spirit, the components of all matter.

MA	stands for matter
THE	stands for theos (Greek: the divine)
MATI	stands for the connecting link between matter and the spiritual or the Divine: the spirit

For biophysics, the most important field of mathematics is geometry. The word Cosmos (Greek: meaning order) alone, indicates that nothing is coincidental.

GEO	represents the Earth and
METRY	corresponds to a unit of measure

Perfect order is inherent in the Divine Creation of Earth.

The three distinct forms of water: solid, liquid, and gaseous

The Various States of Matter

Water is a good example for showing how matter is transformed when energy is added. Water has three different distinct bodies or states: solid, liquid and gaseous. Ice is frozen water. We can see it and feel its coolness. By adding energy in the form of heat to the ice it transforms back into water. We can observe this process. When we add more energy to the water it begins to boil, and the molecules start moving so fast that they transform into steam and become gaseous. However, we can no longer perceive this form of water, except for those particles condensed into clouds. If we would point to the air proclaiming there was water, those who were not part of our experiment would look at us in disbelief. Yet it exists in its most subtle form, as we inhale it with each and every breath.

We tend to believe that what we cannot perceive with our senses does not exist

The Geometric Form Determines the Energy Content

Matter comes into existence by the decrease or slowing of energy. The different energy forms (for example: water can be solid, fluid or gaseous), are changed into a specific form according to

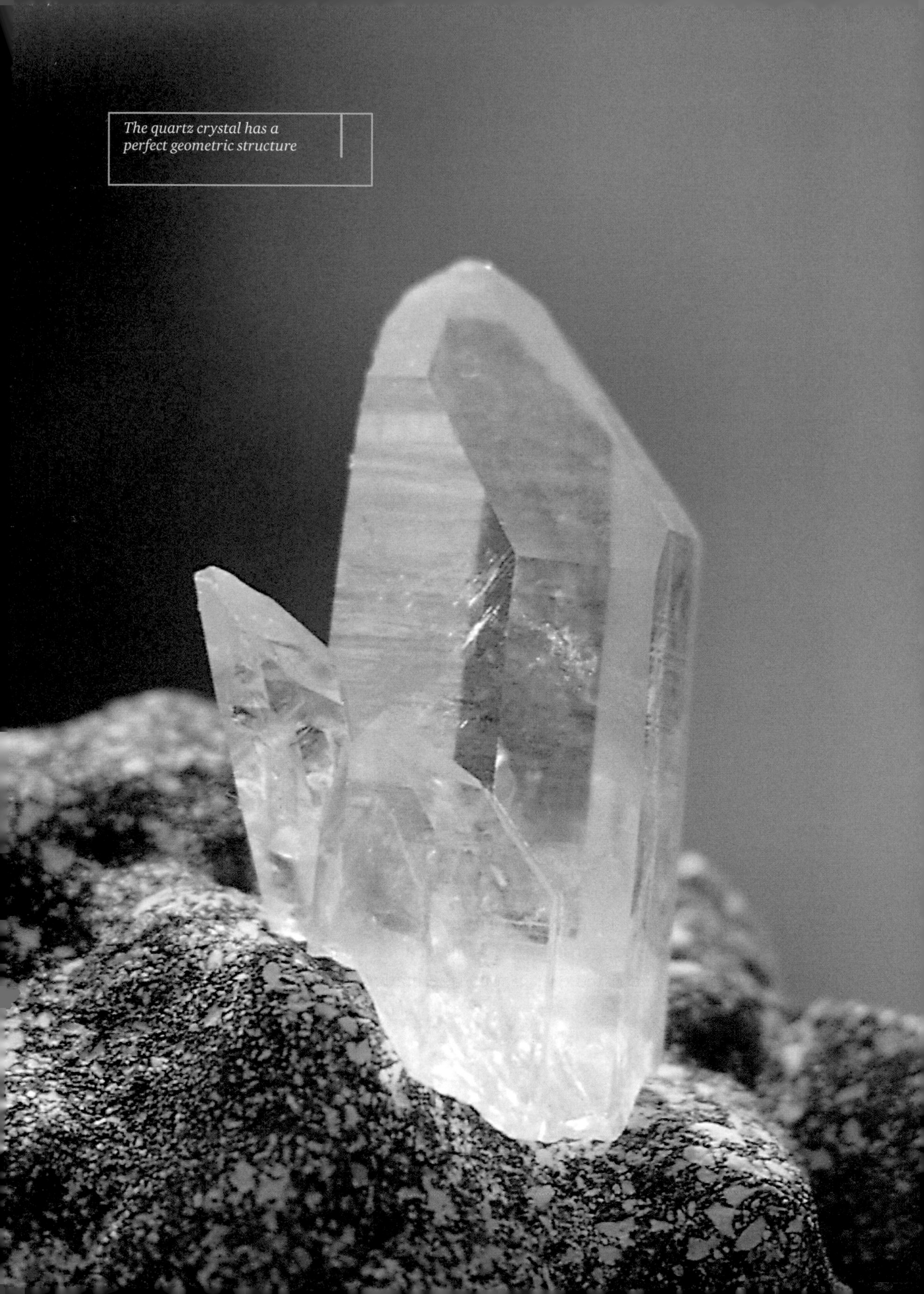

The quartz crystal has a perfect geometric structure

principles of order and of information content. The earliest form of materialized energy, that is, of solid molecular matter on this Earth, is found in the mineral kingdom. Every quartz crystal reflects identical, perfect geometry according to these principles of order. Every crystal has the same trigonal structure and is part of the five known platonic bodies from which all forms of matter arise. So how is it possible that nature, assumed to have come about accidentally, has always given a quartz crystal the same, perfect geometric shape for millions of years?

The Life-Force of Matter

What kind of force, in the form of energy, lies behind this geometrical perfection? When we examine a quartz crystal we find it contains a measurable electric charge. In physics, this kind of power is called piezo-electricity. By now we know that electricity equals energy and energy is synonymous with Life-Force. This makes sense, because as crystals grow they use energy, which is life. Hence, we can speak of the life of a crystal. This also makes every crystal a carrier of information, as we can see in the main element of a computer, the microchip, which is made of quartz crystal. This quartz crystal can only receive, store and transmit information by virtue of its geometric structure. If we would destroy the structure of the crystal, it would, from a chemical standpoint, remain silicate. However, with the annihilation of its physical structure, its information content would be lost. So we can see that it is not the matter, in this case the silicate, that is responsible for the existence of energy content, but its geometrical shape.

Where there is energy flow, there is life. This is also true for the seemingly rigid realm of crystals

The Meaning of the Word Crystal

Have you ever thought how the word crystal came about?

One part of the word derives from the Greek term "Kristos" or "Christos", as in "Christ", meaning "the Anointed One." Anointed means that one is put in "oil," German "OEL", where oil, coming from "OL" means Spirit and "EL" meaning Light. The one with spiritual light, or having raised his consciousness by being initiated into the Light.

However, the word Kristos is much older than Christianity and actually means, in its original definition, consciousness.

That's why the human body of Jesus, because of his consciousness, was called the Anointed One, as those who were anointed were initiated into the metaphysical science of the cosmos.

He, who was anointed, was initiated into the metaphysical laws of the cosmos. It is also the purpose of our life to raise our consciousness to a level of all-consciousness, or "Cryst-Al", "Christ-All", Crystal.

The word "Cryst-Al" means "All-Consciousness"

The Five Platonic Bodies

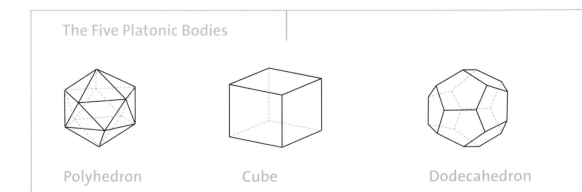

Polyhedron

Cube

Dodecahedron

The Secret of the Pyramids

The ancient high cultures already knew about the indwelling forces-energy/life-force/information/consciousness. Let's take the Egyptians as an example. Isn't it interesting that we can find all of our scientific understanding of mathematics, geometry, physics, astronomy and even astrology, represented in the Pyramids? And that, to this day, we cannot explain with our materialistically inclined intellect, how it was possible for this ancient culture, with their limited means and possibilities at the time, to conceptualize, let alone build, such perfect structures?

But why did the Egyptians and other high cultures put so much time and effort into building these pyramids? Were they really just tombs, as we are taught in school? Couldn't it be possible that they served as initiating centers, to utilize the geometry of the electromagnetic frequency pattern of the building in order to enhance the consciousness of the living being within?

Just tombs, or much more? One thing is certain: the Pyramids are energy centers

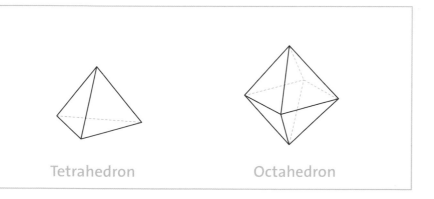

Tetrahedron   Octahedron

Did the ancient Egyptians use the geometrical structure of the Pyramids as energy centers?

The Power of Geometry

The example indicates the energetic powers in the geometry of a pyramid

Let's use an example to illustrate this theory. We can make some very interesting discoveries when we build a small open pyramid structure using eight copper rods according to the geometrical laws of the Cheops Pyramid – hereby we must abide to the exact measure of the length and angles as well as aligning it to its north-south gradient. When we cut a piece of meat in half and place one piece underneath the pyramid and the other outside of it, the piece inside the structure will dehy-drate, whereas the piece of meat outside of it will rot. Or, place a dull razor blade under the pyramid and you will discover, after 60 hours, that is has become sharp again. How is this possible? This is not magic, but rather the alignment of electro-magnetic fields, created by the geometry of the pyramid. A chemist would only search for the effect having come from the particular material being used to build this pyramid. Howe-ver, when he examines the unassembled copper rods, he will not be able to find the source of these effects, he would only find unassembled copper rods.

Energy and Information

Energy and information are identical.

Every form of energy represents a specific wavelength.

Every wavelength has its individual content of information.

There are no accidents in the cosmic order.

Every form of energy strives, due to its information content, to manifest according to a specific principle order.

Every form of matter is the sum of all its inherent information, which follows an impulse from a higher order.

Hence, it is not the matter itself that is responsible for its energy content, but its geometry.

Specific geometric structures, like crystals and pyramids, because of their specific frequency patterns, have specific regulated power.

Health and Disease from a Biophysics Point of View

In biophysics, disease is defined as an energy deficit. Lets go back to the crystals for a moment because these are of cardinal importance for the right understanding of water and salt. How do crystals form? The most beautiful crystals are usually found in the mountains. Tectonic movement creates pressure that forms crystals. When sufficient pressure is exerted on ordinary coal, it creates a geometrically perfect diamond with its own innate energy or information content.

Similarly, our bodies, when healthy, have perfect geometric crystalline structures. If this state is not found in our body, then we are lacking information/energy. The body will then put pressure on us, mostly in the form of suffering, manifesting as disease. When confronted with disease, we are more or less forced to make a change in our life. Our body is telling us that we are lacking something.

In nature, only tremendous pressures are capable of forming perfect geometrical structures

Lack of Energy Causes Disease

What we lack is energy! The simplest and most logical action at this point would be to find out which form of energy we are lacking and, in order to bring our body back into balance, replenish it with the appropriate energy/information. What does this realization tell us? We are in a healthy state when we have sufficient power/energy/information/life-force, as all are equivalent. Let's look at our body as a rechargeable battery. If our body is to function well, we must make sure our batteries are charged. If this is not the case, our natural regulatory mechanism, the homeostasis, doesn't have enough energy to recharge itself and cannot function. So, we can refer to disease as a lack of energy/vitality/information.

To be ill means to lack physical balance, which means a lack of energy

As of today, we know about 40,000 different diseases that are treated by the 1,200 different allopathic specialty fields with 58,000 different kinds of allopathic preparations or medicines at hand. However, the word diseases in the plural form, is not accurate. Have you ever heard of "healths"? We are either healthy or ill. This illness signals a lack of energy and shows up in the form of a symptom. However, to represent a symptom as an illness is technically inaccurate. The symptom is merely the intelligent crying of an energetically defective and suffering body for help. And normally, the body turns to a weakened organ to give us a hint, by means of a symptom, that things are not in order.

Suppressing Symptoms Does Not Heal

An energy deficit creates a chaotic state in the body. Order becomes chaos. If we suppress our symptoms we will not find the cause for our illness, and will not be able to balance our system. This form of treatment is not only ineffective, but can give rise to even worse diseases. Imagine, for example, that the oil indicator light in your car starts blinking, signaling that the car needs oil – a smart invention of the automobile industry to prevent irreparable damage. According to traditional allopathic medicine, treating symptoms rather than the cause of illness, you would just stick a piece of chewing gum over the annoying, blinking oil indicator light so that you could continue to drive without distraction. But how far would you get? After a number

Not the symptoms,
but the cause of
the illness must
be removed

of miles your car would break down. Not because of the red blinking light – which is still blinking; you just can't see it anymore – but because the motor has been damaged beyond repair, as the actual cause of the problem was not dealt with. This means that when you are experiencing symptoms of an illness, you are being shown that you have a deficit in energy and that you must tackle the source of this deficit instead of removing the symptoms of it.

Healing Through Consciousness

Pure energy in its original form is always immaterial and cannot be seen by the human eye. So, for some people, it is easier and seems to make more sense to take a pill than to examine and uncover the potentially far more complex causes of their illness, their energy deficit. However, suppressing the symptoms with medication only adds to the blockage of energy flow (commonly known as harmful side effects about which we are cautioned). If we instead gain conscious insight about the cause of our illness, we actually could replenish the lacking energy. From that point on it is only a matter of time for the homeostasis, the self-regulating mechanisms of the body, to set in and to begin to work again. Through our own power, our body restores itself to its original state of order. This is called healing. If we are capable of balancing the energy level of our body, it will automatically regenerate the affected area, e.g., the organ, into its natural, healthy state. Hence it is obviously neither the doctor nor the therapist that heals us. Not a single one of the 58,000 known alliopathic medications is known to actually heal an illness. Healing happens from within us because healing is a process of consciousness. By becoming conscious, we receive the missing information, the energy, a specific range or pattern of electromagnetic vibrations. This could be through the intake of food, which is gross matter or through subtle food, like words or information from a good thera-pist. But the food or the words of the therapist are only the carriers of information and not the ener-gy itself.

Each word we speak has an energy associated with it. When we speak good or ill of someone, our words carry a vibration pattern of either dissonant or sympathetic frequencies. These waves travel to the one of whom we're speaking, and, like waves breaking on the shore, overwhelm the individual. But we don't recognize, according to a universal of action and reaction, that those very waves we sent to another return to us, still colored with the same, original vibration pattern. In the end, we affect our own self with the energy we send out to others, negative or positive. Remember, we are all interconnected. Maybe that's why our parents told us as children not to talk badly about anyone.

A trusting and open talk with a therapist can also provide healing energy

Illness from a Biophysical Point of View:

Illness is nothing more than an energy deficit.

Symptoms alert us to an illness in our body.

An ill body is not healed by the treatment of its symptoms, but by the replacement of its energy deficit.

Healing occurs by supplying the missing energy in the form of information, bringing about conscious insight, balancing the deficit.

A basic rule for
our diet:
Food can only
give us its life
forces when we
conserve its
vitality

Food from a Biophysical Point of View

Let's take a look at the essence of the word food in general terms (and the German meaning of the word food) before we embark upon our discussion about the two most important food substances for the human body – water and salt. The German word for food is Lebensmittel, which literally translates to "means of life" or "transmitter" or "conveyer of life". Food carries substance; it is a carrier of life force/energy/information/consciousness. But what happens when food looses its life force through various methods of preparation, by chemical alteration or deconstruction? In actuality, food no longer is a "conveyer of life," but becomes instead, a "conveyer of death." Even when, from its chemical structure, it is still made of the identical matter as prior to its preparation.

Food is primarily a carrier of information

From Living Food to Dead Food

The famous Oxford studies demonstrate in a most impressive way what happens to food when it gets changed through processing. Scientists analyzed cow's milk from both a chemical and biophysical aspect. From a biochemical aspect they saw that the milk had a very high calcium and protein content. They checked the electromagnetic frequency pattern in the lower frequencies. By doing so, they found that the milk had a natural, holistic structure (the orderly structure of the elements creates a blueprint), where different frequency patterns of an energy spectrum could be detected. From a biochemical viewpoint, the detected elements, like calcium and protein, are of great importance. The biochemist talks of the importance of calcium for building bones in the baby calf and of the protein necessary for its muscle growth. After this analysis, the milk was pasteurized. After analyzing the pasteurized milk

Pasteurization destroys the information content of milk

they found that it still contained the same calcium and protein. From a chemical standpoint, the milk hadn't changed and it could still be fed to the calf because it contained all the essential elements. However, when this pasteurized milk was fed to a calf for three weeks, it died.

How is this possible, if, chemically viewed, the chemical nutrients were intact? What changes were introduced in the milk by this treatment, causing the calf's death?

Through pasteurizing, the crystalline structure of the milk was destroyed, resulting in the destruction of its inherent geometric structure. As a result, there couldn't be detected any energy at all, or only a totally altered form of energy. The milk was no longer alive.

When Eating Food costs Energy

Food is much more than the sum of its chemical components

The original, organic calcium became inorganic due to its processing, which changed the structure/information. In order for the calcium to be assimilated in the intestines, it must be in its organic form. Otherwise, it becomes more of a burden to the body because it no longer supports the metabolism and the body must use its own calcium reserves. Studies with school children showed that those who drank a lot of milk had the poorest teeth and weakest bone structure. If we eat dead food instead of living food, the body gets only empty calories and no information. Instead of receiving energy and vitality, the body has to draw on its own remaining energy to digest and discard the dead food. Although we have eaten food, we have actually robbed the body of its energy instead of adding to its supply.

Deadly Radiation from the Microwave

A scientific study done in England examined the effects that conventional microwave cooking has on our food. The study revealed the following: A group of cats were kept in a room with artificial light and fed exclusively foods and water that had been heated in a microwave oven. The animals had an abundant variety of food choices. However, they all died within a month. What was the cause of their death? They died of hunger, although they were constantly eating. The short wave radiation of the microwave changed the molecular structure of the food. And it altered it to such an extent that not only could no feasible resonant energy be measured, but also the chemical structure of the food had been changed.

If you have a microwave oven at home you can perform a simple experiment. Take a piece of bread with a slice of cheese and microwave it, not for 30 seconds, but for a few minutes. You will discover that the cheese will not only look and taste like plastic, but that it has actually undergone a chemical change and is, chemically, now almost similar to plastic. The molecular structures of the elements were actually changed. A substance was entirely changed into another one, having nothing in common with its original state.

Food in its Original State is Best

From a biophysical perspective, food is only a carrier of information to the body. This vital information is important to a healthy diet. Eat vital foods, foods that are alive, and alter your food as little as possible so that the holistic body is not destroyed. If we extract vitamin C from an acerola cherry in the belief that we will receive natural vitamin C instead of synthetic, we have to consider that we have changed the holistic body of the fruit, and with this, also, its information content that was to be delivered to us via the vitamin C. This perspective forces us to look deeper into food supplements and sheds a new light on the perceived value derived from their use.

When we plant an apple seed it will grow into an apple tree. A grain will also bring a new stalk into life, containing more

Processed food is dead food and robs the body of energy

If the molecular structure of food is changed, the energy content is destroyed

grains. Try the same with apple butter and corn chips and you can wait for eternity. They will never be able to produce life because both are dead material. An untreated, natural apple

contains, in the biophysical sense, more energy and information content than all the cooked food we eat in the course of a day.

The Right Diet from a Biophysical Perspective

If you start your day with fresh fruit or wholemeal you will have an abundance of energy for your daily routine. Eat your vegetables either raw or slightly steamed instead of cooking them to death. In this way you will maintain the valuable structure, and with it, the energy content. Try to eat more alkaline foods because over acidity is the cause of many ills of the body. A balanced diet is composed of 75% alkaline and 25% acidic food. In general, alkaline foods include fruits, vegetables, greens and spelt. Acidic foods include grains (except spelt), meat, fish, eggs, milk products, animal fats, coffee, tea and alcohol.

Generally speaking, we should be careful with animal protein intake. It's difficult for our digestion system to assimilate cow's milk, because we lack the necessary enzymes. Therefore, our body is restricted in receiving and benefiting from the valuable calcium, vitamins and amino acid. And, as we discussed previously, the milk is being pasteurized and homogenized and its energy and information content has been destroyed.

Why Vegans have no Deficiencies

A research study of 8,000 people who choose the vegan diet, which abstains from all animal protein, like milk, meat, fish, and egg, has shown that they had sufficient vitamin B12, although it is said that vitamin B12 can only be found in animal proteins and that the human body cannot produce it on its own. But maybe it can.

In nutrition, it's not so much about the presence or absence of vitamin B12, but about the body's ability, given the proper energy, to be able to put back the elements of which it consists into a specific geometrical and molecular structure. This molecular structure consists of what we call, in chemical terms, vitamin B12. A vitamin is nothing but a molecular grouping of different elements which can already found or are inherent in our body. It's not the vitamin B12 itself which makes it so valuable to our body, but its ability to transmit information, according to its molecular geometry.

Eat mainly living and alkaline foods, and be moderate with animal proteins!

Coming Back into Balance

To live a healthy life you do not have to become a vegan. However, it is recommended that we pay more attention to what we eat and drink and be especially sensitive to the vitality of our food. Our body is more able to adapt to the ever-changing environmental influences if it has enough energy. To a certain extent, we are able to detoxify and discharge toxins and keep them from being deposited in our system, by virtue of the orderly structure of our blood.

With the proper energy balance we are even able to repair certain malfunctions in our body. But each single case must be looked upon from a cause-and-effect viewpoint. According to the principle of energy, every alteration or change of matter can be transformed back to its original state by adding the missing energy with its information. It's only a question of time and perseverance to re-establish this state of balance. Take some time to help your body regain its normal balance. Be conscious of the energy that your body needs to function optimally and try to eat more living foods as a part of you diet. In this way your body will gradually, once again, become balanced.

If we have sufficient energy, we will stay healthy and strong

A Healthy Diet

Food is a carrier of information/life-force.

When the geometrical structure of food is altered, its information/living energy is altered or destroyed as well.

Raw, unaltered plant foods are the fundamentals of a healthy diet.

A healthy diet should consist of primarily alkaline foods.

A good diet can help to balance energy deficits and repair malfunctions in the body.

Table of Acids and Bases

Vegetables, Salads, Herbs, Fungi	+/−
Kale	+
Red cabbage	++
Rhubarb	++
Leek tuber	++
Leek leaves	+++
Beans	++
Boletus	+
Chanterelle	+
Mushroom	+
Water cress	++
Dill	++
Chives	++
Zucchini	++
Asparagus	+
Onion	+
Cauliflower	+
Savoy cabbage	+
Peas	++
Spinach	+++
Celery	+++
Tomato	+++
Lamb's lettuce	+
Endive	+++
Dandelion	+++++
Cucumber	+++++++
Butterhead lettuce	+++
Chicory	++++
Brussels sprout	− −
Artichoke	−

Potatoes, Root Vegetables	+/−
Black salsify	+
Radish, black	++++++
Radish, white	+
Potato	++
Turnip cabbage	+
Horseradish	++
Carrot	++
Beetroot	+++

Fruit	+/−
Apple	+
Black currant	++
Strawberry	+
Pear	+
Cherry	+
Sour cherry	+
Pineapple	+
Date	+
Banana	++
Yellow plum	+
Prune	+
Raspberry	+
Mango	+
Melon	+
Bilberry	++
Plum	++
Peach	++
Apricot	++
Cranberry	++
Blackberry	++
Grape	++
Gooseberry	++
Orange	++
Lemon	++
Tangerine	+++
Raisin	+++
Rose hip	+++
Fig	++++++

Please note: All canned fruit are acid-forming, because of their high sugar ratio. Deep-frozen fruit and vegetables that have not been processed beforehand, largely retain the indicated values.

Dairy products, Eggs	+/−
Cow's milk	+
Buttermilk	+
Goat's milk	+
Whey	+
Sheep's milk	+
Soy milk	+
Hard cheese	− − − −
Yoghurt	− − − −
Curd	− − − −
Cream	+ −
UHT-milk	−
Hen's egg	− − − − − −

Flour, Pasta, Grains	+/−
Potato starch	+
Lenses	++
White beans	+++
Soy flour	+++
Soy beans	++++
Bean sprouts	+++++
Rice	− − − − − −
Paddy	− − −
Rice starch	−
Rye flour	− − − −
Pearl barley	− − −
Wheat flour	−
Wheat semolina	− −
Noodles	−
Oatmeal	− −

Bread, Cake, Sweets	+/−
Spelt bread	+ −
Brown bread	− − −
White bread	− −
Zwieback	− −
Wholewheat bread	− −
Crispbread	−
Sugar	− − − − − −
Cake	− − − − − −
Chocolate	− − − − − −
Sweetmeat	− − − − − −

Meat, Fish, Sausage	+/−
Lamb	− −
Pork	− − − − − −
Veal	− − − − − −
Beef	− − − − − −
Seawater fish	− − − −
Freshwater fish	− − −
Turkey hen	− −
Chicken	− −
Goose and duck	− − −
Ham	− − − − − −
Fresh sausages	− − − − − −
Peperoni	− − − − − −
Turkey hen's ham	− −

Nut, Seeds	+/−
Peanut	− − −
Brazil nut	− −
Walnut	− −
Pumpkin seed	+
Sunflower seed	+
Chest nut	+ −
Almond	+ −
Hazel-nut	+ −
Cashew nuts	+ −
Pitachio	+ −

Fats	+/−
Margarine	− −
Butter	−
Olive oil, cold-pressed	+

Beverages	+/−
Coffee	− − − −
Black tea	− − − −
Alcohol	− − − − −
Cola	− − − − −
Lemonade	− − − − − −
Freshly squeezed fruit juices	++
Vegetable juices	++
Mineral water, carbon.	− −
Spring water, non-carbon.	+ −
Herb tea	++

weakly basic	+
strongly basic	++++++
weakly acidic	−
strongly acidic	− − − − − −
neutral	+ −

The

Water

The Pillar of Life

Water is the pillar of all life forms. It is the beginning and the end of a life cycle. Our life and our health, as well as the life and health of our planet, are completely dependent upon water. All life forms on Earth come from the primal oceans. About seventy percent of the planet is covered with water. If we look at our planet Earth from space and compare that image with a water molecule under a microscope, we will find a surprising resemblance. Water penetrates through all cells in the body and enables communication between cell clusters. Water regulates all functions of the organism, like our body's construction, metabolism, digestion and circulation, to name a few. Beyond the physical realms, water is responsible for our consciousness, because it empowers our thought processes, feelings and moods. Water is the carrier of all physical and mental (i.e. non-physical) information.

> Water is not only important for our physical body, but is also responsible for our thought processes, feelings, and moods

The Functions of Water in our Body

Beyond its biophysical life-giving effect, water is also, chemically, a solvent, transporter and cleanser. Throughout the metabolism, it facilitates cleansing, the transport of nutrients and the removal of waste products; furthermore, it maintains the osmotic pressure of the cells and regulates the body temperature. All metabolic procedures rely on water to function. The same is true for extracting toxins through the kidneys, the colon, the skin and the lungs. Within a time period of twenty-four

Drink at least two quarts of pure water every day

hours, about three hundred and seventy gallons of blood flows through our brain. In the same amount of time, about five hundred and thirty gallons of blood passes through our kidneys. On a daily basis the human body discharges about 0.4 to 0.6 gallons of water; this perpetual loss of liquid needs to be constantly replenished. The amount of water our body needs depends upon our weight. The rule of thumb is to drink about half an ounce of water per pound of body weight. For example, if you weigh one hundred and thirty pounds, then your daily water intake should be roughly two quarts.

Drink at Least Two Quarts of Water Every Day

Adequate daily intake of high quality water is of paramount importance. With the starvation of the body for water comes the expiration of our cells. The more our bodies are starved for water, the greater the number of cells that will die. Dehydration follows, and the process of aging is accelerated. Drink at least two quarts of water every day. This means pure water, not coffee, tea, wine, beer or soda. The fewer ingredients (including minerals) the water contains the better, because water has a flushing function. Mineral waters or carbonated waters are saturated and can no longer absorb toxins.

Water has an even more important function. Water is not just a material substance with specific scientifically proven qualities and capacities. Water is a vital force, upon which all life depends. Water is a carrier of energy and information. But how can this natural element, water, perform all these amazing functions?

If we drink enough water, our body can eliminate toxins much quicker

Water – An Extraordinary Element

To date, modern scientists have yet to perform much research on water. The formula H_2O defines water chemically, but it doesn't say anything about its inherent nature. From a biochemical and biophysical point of view, water is an anomaly, because it behaves in ways that scientist don't expect it to. The boiling point of water, according to physical law, should be as low as 114.8°F. However, it boils at 212°F. When water freezes and becomes solid, it expands instead of contracting in volume, as would be expected. At 98.6°F, which is our body's normal temperature, water has its lowest specific heat. At this temperature the greatest amount of energy is needed to effect a change in the temperature. This abnormal physical behavior of water plays a central role in life on Earth, because, in fact, it enables the existence of life. If water would behave normally in only one aspect, there would be no life on Earth.

The Structure of Water

Minerals were the first to appear on this Earth, and, like all forms of matter, they are based on a geometric structure. Water, as matter, also has a specific geometric form: a tetrahedron, which represents one of the five platonic bodies found in nature. This form is the reason that we can say that water is, in fact, a liquid crystal. Chemically, water consists of two parts hydrogen and one part oxygen (H_2O). The tetrahedral angle representing the water molecule is one-hundred-four-point-seven (104.7) degrees. Considering that it is energy that transforms the water molecule from its original state of vibration into a state of matter, it is interesting to note that four water molecules, which are actually four tetrahedrons in their combined alignment, form the precise structure of the great pyramids.

Maybe the ancient Egyptians had something in mind by using the platonic bodies of the elements as the central idea in constructing their monuments?

Individual water molecules form clusters. The connections between the H2O molecules are called hydrogen bridges. There are innumerable ways in which these bridges are built and, as such, suggest a vast array of possibilities for building structures which are liquid, yet crystalline. Because it is the geometric structure that is responsible for specific electromagnetic frequency patterns, distinct wavelengths can also be measured in water. The cluster formations enable water to store information. This is the underlying basic principle behind homeopathic remedies, such as Bach flower essences, gem stone essences

Water can be called a crystal because it has the geometric structure of a tetrahedron

work, or other forms of homeopathy. Hildegard von Bingen, the German mystic of the Middle Ages, suggested to place gemstones with specific energy patterns in water, to drink for healing purposes. Today, her intuitive understanding can be proven through biophysical research.

The Uniqueness of the Water Molecule

An individual water molecule's uniqueness, or dissimilarity to any other water molecule, is best demonstrated in a snowflake under a microscope. Each has its own unique and perfect geometric structure. What principle of creation is concealed within these fascinating constructions? What forces, what dynamics, cause these crystalline shapes to form? Even though they are all based on the same crystalline structure, no two snowflakes are exactly the same. If snowflakes were only the sum of its chemical parts, two parts hydrogen and one part oxygen, as their chemical definition suggests, they would all have identical physical characteristics, looking exactly the same. However, it is the energy responsible for building matter by slowing down the vibration enough, which forms these crystalline structures.

The Memory of Water

If a snowflake is melted and then refrozen under the same natural conditions, it reforms into the exact same snowflake. Water has memory. The snowflake remembers what it is. Every water molecule has its own unmistakable identity. It is energy that forms matter, not the other way around!

Water is more than simply H_2O. Work in the field of photon research has revealed remarkable discoveries. It takes more than one billion light quanta to build only one single water molecule. This complements the discoveries of the Swiss atomic physicist and Nobel Prize winner, Dr. Carlo Rubbia. He was able to demonstrate through a mathematical ratio, that it takes more than one billion energy units in order to manifest a single unit of matter. Photons are pure light energy. They align each and every single water molecule in their own unique way and give each its unmistakable identity (exactly as with human beings).

Not one water molecule is the same as another. We can see these molecules clearly under an electron microscope in their frozen state. Here are three photos of possible ice crystal formations

If we apply this information to our physical body, this insight suggests that organs in our body can only change when the energy that manifests, and is continuously supporting the manifestation of the organ, changes. If this change results in an energy deficit, we become ill. However, if we give our body the correct information, it will be able to heal itself again.

Due to its crystalline structure, water is able to store and transfer information

The Power of Information in Water

But water can do even more: it can transfer frequency patterns/wavelengths to us. When we throw a stone into water we create a wave that expands outward, in a circle. It also expands in volume, because the wave moves through the water's depth. Because of the structure of water, it can pass information on to us. When two similar wavelengths superimpose, with the exact same frequency and coming from different sources, in scientific terms this is called the resonant effect. Resonant wavelengths create order, as seen in quartz crystals.

Quartz crystals resonate with the universe and have come into manifestation as perfect geometric forms according to a natural

Along with the motion of the waves, information is spread throughout the water

order or law. The opposite of resonance is dissonance. Dissonance is created when the polarities of the frequencies don't match. Other terms for these disharmonic vibrations include entropy or chaos and they act in a destructive manner. We humans share the same phenomena of resonance. When we feel very familiar with someone, when we fall in love or have the feeling that we want to merge with another person, we express ourselves with respective phrases: "We're on the same wavelength" or "We have chemistry" or "We vibe well together." Conversely, we also know that there are those with whom we do not share common wavelengths. Just as it is among human beings, it is with every other element, with every forming molecular compound. Our body, from a physical perspective, is nothing but a sum of elements that come together as molecules in order to build a specific geometrical structure.

Only waves with the same length create perfect harmony

The Power of the Spoken Word

The prominent Japanese scientist Dr. Masaru Emoto performed interesting experiments within the last 10 years: He spoke to water. More specifically, he spoke different messages to the water, which afterwards he froze at 23°F and then photographed. Water imprinted with the information "You make me sick" showed a chaotic structure similar to a cancerous ulcer. He then melted that same water and spoke the word "love" to it. When photographed after being refrozen at 23°F, it had become a perfect geometric crystalline structure. This shows that even words can be "living food" or "dead food." We all know the power of words. Words are the spoken manifestation of our thoughts. We also know how damaging words can be. One single word can have such an impact on us that we cannot forgive or forget it for the rest of our life. On one hand, our thoughts and words have the power to make others euphoric and give them courage to live and on the other hand they

The Japanese scientist Dr. Masaru Emoto experiments with water as a carrier of information

Ice crystal from the holy source of Lourdes in France, also called Source of Miracles

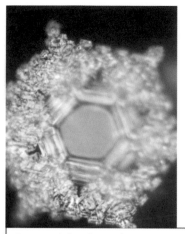

Ice crystal that the word "love" was spoken to

Water, the structure of which was destroyed when told "You make me sick"

also have the power to scare people to death. Our words have the power to create or destroy.

When Other People Make us Sick

Negative thoughts also have a negative effect on human beings because they destroy our crystalline structure

Even if we were living the healthiest lifestyle, we would still become ill if there were people who constantly tell us "You make me sick." Words can have such a destructive effect on us that other people, with their negative thoughts and words directed at us, can literally dig our graves. Hence, not only do our good deeds matter but also our good thoughts and good words. By first having good thoughts, good words and good deeds will follow naturally. Seventy percent of our body is water. The water of which we are composed is a crystal, which is carrying information. And thanks to its liquid state it is able to continually adapt to the constant changes in our environment, whether they be positive or negative. Just as water can absorb and store positive information, it can do the same with

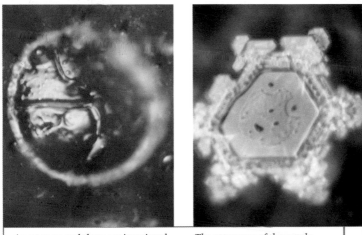

A water crystal that was imprinted with the name "Adolf Hitler"

The utterance of the words "Mother Teresa" enabled the same water to revert to a perfect crystalline structure

negative information. This is where modern technologies, applied to clean our water, fall short. Filtering, distillation or reverse osmosis technologies can clear the water of most toxins, etc.; however they fail to remove the pollutants' destructive energetic vibrations!

The destructive impregnation of water by pollutants cannot be removed merely through technology

The Abilities of Water

Water is the source of all life.

Water stores and transmits information.

Water manages all functions of the body, from metabolism to cognition.

Water is a carrier of energy/information/life-force.

Every water molecule has its own unmistakable identity.

The Movement of Water

Water never flows
straight but always
in a spiraling fashion

Have you ever observed water flowing in nature? It never flows straight. It spirals. This creates the winding pattern of creeks and rivers. Everywhere in nature and in the cosmos we find centripetal movement, a movement from the outside in, spiraling towards the center of this movement. But because, at the same time, the water molecule is a dipole, it also spirals from the inside out. This same spiral movement happens in our body. Our modern technology works exactly the opposite: centrifugal towards the periphery, explosive as opposed to implosive. However, spiraling movement is an important principle of the cosmos, the definition of which, in fact, means "order." The spiraling movement of water is also called a meander movement. This movement is caused by the Earth's gravitation and universal expansion (levitation). We all know that water flows downward; however, only very few people know that water also flows upward, simultaneously, due to the force of levitation. It is this force of levitation that enables spring water to bubble to the surface, finding daylight, even at the tops of 10,000-foot-high mountains. Water is in a constant state of flowing, it moves continuously as long as it is able to.

The Power of Body Fluids

Water, flowing in the form of bodily fluids like blood or lymph, in a meandering movement through our organism, builds gravitational and levitation forces, which create energy. In our spinal cord, the energies spiral in winding fashion and maintain the electrical current. If water can move freely, it moves up and down in our body, just as it flows within a bottle. Within this context we will speak of blood circulation. In 1912, Nobel Prize winner Alexis Carrel discovered that it is not the heart that is continuously pumping the blood through our veins. The heart, it was discovered, is not a pump with its own little built-in motor. Instead, it is a kind of turbine. Our body fluids activate this turbine. By moving up and down in our body, they give our heart a specific frequency pattern, our pulse.

It's not our heart that is the primary driving force for our circulation, but the forces of levity and gravity that influence our body fluids

The ocean: the ideal place for relaxation and regeneration

In Resonance with the Cosmos

Due to the rhythms of the fluids flowing through our body, we are resonating with the cosmos as a part of the whole. It is the gravitational energies of the water in our body which keep our feet on the ground – otherwise we would be catapulted into space. On the other hand it is also due to the forces of levitation in our body fluids that we are able to arise from our beds every morning. Staying grounded and yet wanting to soar and achieve something in life – if this ratio of powers is not in harmony and we no longer resonate with nature, we experience dissonance, an unbalanced state of being.

If the force of gravity predominates on our bodily fluids, then the influential weight of the water that our body contains, literally pulls us to the ground. Lying flat on our backs is another way of saying that we are ill. We can no longer stand on our feet, because there is not sufficient levitation force to remain erect. Only after we regenerate ourselves, by replenishing the energy deficit and restoring the energy balance in our body, we can once again stand on our feet. We have regained our vitality, our life force.

The Journey of Water through the Earth

While water travels through the earth, it absorbs all the electro magnetic vibrations that are present on our planet. Water becomes the "blood of our planet," as the renowned Austrian scientist Victor Schauberger (1885-1958) aptly put it. Just as Earth has a North and a South Pole, every water molecule has a north and a south pole, too. The atmosphere of the Earth corresponds to the electromagnetic field of the individual water molecule. Our Earth's atmosphere vibrates at 7.83 Hertz and is called the Schuhmann Resonance Frequency. Water absorbs this frequency pattern on its journey through the Earth. Our body, in return, has the same frequency pattern as the water molecule. Our brain waves have a frequency of 8-10 Hertz. Water connects us to the Earth's frequency. This also means that, with water, we can replenish what our body is missing when we are ill. Water can balance the energy deficit that causes the illness. That's why we are told to drink plenty of liquids – but really we should only drink pure spring water.

As water flows through the earth, it absorbs all electro magnetic vibrations of our planet

Every civilization has
used the healing
and relaxing
properties of water

Since ancient times people have been utilizing the healing powers of water in the form of thermal bathing or by soaking in hot springs. The successful naturopathic healer, Paracelsus, swore by the healing properties of water. He had the ingenious idea of giving his patients water, warmed to 98.6°F, to drink for their recuperation. Paracelsus was convinced that water, being the "mother of all life," contained everything necessary for

Typical Properties of Water

Water flows in a spiral fashion.

Water flows downward (gravitational), as well as upwards (forces of levitation).

Water is the life-force in our body.

Water absorbs all frequency patterns on its journey through the Earth and stores them.

healing a human being. Doctor Faridum Batmanghelidj, author of the renowned book: "Your Body's Many Cries for Water," has recognized that the cause of many chronic diseases lies in the dehydration of the body. His message is: "You are not sick, you are thirsty." When he was thrown into jail by the Iranian revolutionary government, he healed many of his inmates of a wide spectrum of diseases such as allergies, spinal pain, ulcers of the stomach and even depression, simply by having them drink water! His suggestion is to drink one half-hour before and two-and-a-half hours after a meal. In total, he recommends between two quarts to one gallon of water per day. He also points out the dangers of caffeine, specifically drinks such as coffee and cola, because they dehydrate the body instead of supplying it with liquids!

Parson Kneipp was also convinced that we can reactivate our body's self-healing abilities

What Parson Kneipp Already Knew

The healing properties of water were a keystone for Parson Kneipp, the renowned neuropathic healer from the German spa of Wörishofen. He was convinced that the body itself, in principle, incorporated all necessary healing properties, and that illness would occur only when those properties where blocked. He developed hydrotherapy, a therapy that stimulates the body with heat, cold and pressure in order to retune the body and activate the self-healing forces. In his time, Kneipp was not taken too seriously. But today, one hundred years after his death, his hydrotherapy is very popular. Time-tested remedies are being rediscovered today, such as hot baths for colds when no fever is present, or rising footbaths for urinary infections. Frequent visits to saunas and steam baths have become common preventative health care measures in our society.

Healing with Colon-Hydrotherapy

A modern form of water therapy is colon-hydrotherapy. It detoxifies and cleanses the body in a way that wasn't possible before. Colon-hydrotherapy is a modern version of an enema and cleanses the colon very efficiently. During therapy, warm

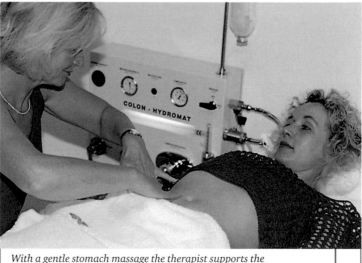

With a gentle stomach massage the therapist supports the soothing effect of colon-hydrotherapy

water is funneled into the colon and removed again. There are apparent benefits here: The entire large intestine is hygienically flushed by a closed system with water or a salt-water solution. With a gentle massage over the stomach and intestines, the colon therapist is able to feel his/her way to the problematic areas where blockages are occurring, and can guide the water into these places. The solvent effect of the water together with the simultaneous warm-cool stimulation of the colon reactivates the colon's ability to pass its contents on its own again. The cleansing of the colon with the hydrotherapy machine is clean and odorless and is described as a pleasant experience by those who have undergone this treatment. Some are even euphoric about the positive effects on their well-being. Following the hydrotherapy treatment, the colon's flora is replenished by taking natural acidophilus.

Colon-Hydrotherapy

A healthy colon–resembling the roots of a tree–is the pillarof a strong, vital and healthy body.

Because of our denatured diet that is low in fibers and additionally compromised by pesticides and heavy metals, problems involving the colon and our digestive system are common.

Waste material that has been stuck in our colon for too longhas the tendency to ferment and decay. This breeds dangerous bacteria, fungi and other poisons.

Colon-Hydrotherapy is odorless and clean and patients havefound it to be pleasant. The entire large intestine is flushed several times by a solid tube system and cleansed of its toxins.

Holy and Healing Water

Natural, living spring water is a natural remedy. But don't drink water just to become healthier. Drink water for its consciousness-expanding purposes as well. Water is consciousness! It is not a coincidence that our brain is ninety percent water. Water is full of living energy and healing information because it gives the body's innate self-healing forces the energy it needs to regenerate and recharge its batteries. This understanding explains the significance of holy springs, such as the holy springs of Fatima and Lourdes, to name a couple. They are considered as holy because their waters are known to heal. Every year about eight million people make a pilgrimage to these sites to drink the holy waters. Over six thousand miracle healings have been documented at Lourdes. However, these so-called miracles can actually be explained scientifically. Specific frequency patterns have been found in the water. In principal, water, because of its geometric structure, is influenced by many factors. First, as the water rises to form clouds, it is infused with solar and atmospheric vibrations. Next, once the rain falls to earth and enters the ground, it becomes impregnated with the geomagnetic frequencies of the Earth. These particular electromagnetic vibrations of the water transmit healing energy to the body. Most holy springs are several hundred years old. It's not surprising. The longer the water remains in the "womb" of "Mother Earth," the greater the potential charging of the water, like a battery when fully charged. Biochemically, the water from Lourdes doesn't differ from the water of vicinal springs which don't have healing properties. However, when we look at these waters biophysically, we can find vast differences: The frequency of the Lourdes water is particularly unique.

It has been scientifically proven that holy waters are healing waters as well

Water – More Than a Thirst Quencher

Drinking water for the sole purpose of hydrating and detoxifying our body shouldn't be our only motivation. We should rather look at water as our primary, most important food source that replenishes us and nourishes us with its necessary living energy and information. This is not esoteric exaggeration, but scientific fact. In Italy there are, as of today, fourteen distinguished, medically recognized "light and water" treatment centers, which confirm a history of exceptional healing successes. But where is the water that still holds such healing properties in our world today? Primarily, these properties can be found in water from artesian springs. The significance of an artesian spring is that the water has surfaced on its own, fully developed without any drilling or man-made pressure. Water requires a stage of maturation. It only surfaces when it carries sufficient forces of levitation to overcome gravity. This levitation power can even overcome the force of gravity, the proof of which can be seen, as natural springs occur in mountains at altitudes exceeding 10,000 feet.

> Only water which surfaces on its own, is truly mature and healthy water

Spring Water is Best

The ideal circumstances would be to have access to a local, natural spring in your vicinity, from which you could fill your own bottles. Perhaps you live in a community where spring water is available for free. Many communities throughout the U.S. have their spring water tested regularly. If you are unsure about the quality of water from a spring, have the water analyzed.

When You Should Drink Water

Drink water between meals: No later than a half to a quarter of an hour before a meal and no sooner than two hours after a meal, in the ideal case. It is suggested to only drink a small amount of liquids with your meal because water and other liquids dilute your digestive fluids and considerably slow down your digestion. Fermentation and putrefaction in your colon are the consequence.

Once you realize where your life energy orginates, you will be more conscious about your drinking water.

There are many private and state agencies that can test water. Although the standards for testing and labeling drinking water vary from state to state, the analysis will expose any potentially harmful impurities in the water. Also, universities often have extension services that can test water samples for you.

Once you begin to think about where your water, your life energy originates, and how important water is to your body's well being, you will start making conscious choices about the water you drink.

The Healing Effects of Water

Water is an energy carrier.

The frequency pattern of water equals that of the Earth and of our brain.

The innate healing properties of water have been known for centuries and are scientifically proven.

Pure spring water is the best water and gives us life-force.

The Quality of Our Water

Supplying healthy drinking water is one of the major problems facing our modern communities, as scores of chemical toxins pollute our environment. Most recent statistics show that, only in America, more than 5 billion pounds of pesticides and fungicides were used in agriculture in 1998-99, of which 280 are scientifically proven to be carcinogenic. Our drinking water still carries up to 300 different kinds of pesticide and fungicide residues. We live with an enormous number of undetected pesticides and fungicides in our drinking water, the names of which we know little, and even less about their minimum acceptable values. When, as it has happened, limits values for pesticides and fungicides were exceeded, governments simply increased those values and reduced of the number of substances which are to be examined.

We live with an enormous number of undetected pesticides and fungicides in our drinking water

Dangerous Calcification

In America there are over 6,500 pesticides, herbicides, and fungicides, and the numbers of these products continue to increase. Water pollution varies heavily from community to community. We have technology to clean the water from toxins and bacteria, with the help of water treatment plants. Bio-chemically, we basically end up with purified drinking water. But all you have to do in order to realize that there's something wrong with our drinking water is to fill some water inside your electric teakettles and let it boil. The calcium that you find accumulating in this and other household appliances naturally accumulates in our body, particularly in our vessels. We fill our electric irons with distilled water in order to prolong their life span. But what about our bodies? If we want to avoid calcium accumulation in our body, we must drink "living water" that is low in minerals.

Tap Water from a Biophysical Perspective

Water pipes destroy the crystalline structure of water, which destroys its living energy

From a biophysical point of view, the quality of our tap water, which is meant to be fit for consumption, suffers from another serious downfall: the fact that it is delivered to us through pipes. About 260 feet of pipeline transportation is already sufficient to destroy the natural flow of water and its crystalline structure. Under the pressure in the pipes the natural structure of the water molecules collapses. Our tap water has lost most of its natural geometrical information, and therefore most of its information content. And this is the primary purpose for drinking water in the first place: we absolutely need to drink water to receive its information and its living energy.

Another important aspect arises in this context has been demonstrated by the biophysicist Dr. Wolfgang Ludwig. Water treatment removes chemically most of the pollutants, such as lead, cadmium and nitrate. However, most people don't know that the chemically clean water still carries certain magnetic frequencies, which an analysis proves to derive from the very pollutants that have been removed. This means the water still carries the memory of the pollutants, similar to a negative imprint, which can be detrimental to our health. In spite of the chemical treatment of water that is contaminated with heavy metals, the dissonant vibrations of the heavy metals are still present in the water and are transmitted to our body. So even if our water is chemically clean, it is physically polluted all the same. It is not the chemical substance that affects the physical body in this instance, it is the dissonant, chaos-causing frequency patterns.

Our body needs the information held in water

Does Water Affect Our Willpower?

The purification of our water by adding fluoride and chlorine poses another danger. Chlorine causes an unnatural isolated frequency pattern in our body, which promotes dissonant thought patterns in our brain. Science has known for about seventy years that sodium fluoride damages a certain region of the brain, an area where our individual willpower or self-assertion resides. This willpower is evidently surrendered after long-term consumption of tap water and common table salt. Think of how many people have been drinking water treated with fluoride and eating common table salt for thirty years or longer. It comes as no surprise that there are so many consumer slaves in our society, materialistic and without any willpower. As long as there is sufficient energy in our body, we can liberate ourselves from such negative information in water. However, if we consume this kind of water every day, it is only a matter of time until our body falls out of its state of order and becomes ill. The poor condition of our drinking water must be seen as one of the main causes for the dramatic increase of diseases. Considering the quality of our tap water, it's not surprising that more and more people are buying drinking water, especially mineral waters, in order to avoid contamination and to boost or increase their mineral intake. But can we absorb the minerals contained in mineral waters?

The poor condition of our drinking water must be seen as one of the foremost causes for the dramatic increase of diseases

Mineral Waters under Scrutiny

First we must differentiate between inorganic minerals, those that come directly from the soil, and organically bound minerals. Plants can absorb inorganic components from the soil through photosynthesis (transformation of light energy into nutrition), and transform them into organically bound minerals. These are bound to the geometric structure of the plant

Our bodies cannot absorb the minerals from mineral water, as they are much too coarse

juice. Plant juice holds the same surface tension as our blood and, therefore, is one of the best fluids for our body. In its perfect, natural, whole state, unaltered plant juice is an exceptionally valuable food. Human beings, by nature, are "frugivores" fruit and grain eaters. Ideally, fruits and grains should be eaten, if possible, exactly the way they are found in nature. These foods are composed of pure light. The human cells are not able to absorb inorganic minerals directly. The plant cells must either metabolize them first, to transform them into an organic structure, or they must be introduced in a colloidal form (composed of extremely fine particles that do not dissolve in other substances). The minerals found in mineral water, however, are

mostly too coarse to be absorbed by our body. Even worse, when the water is "dead," it prevents our body from passing toxins. In general, the fewer minerals a water contains, the greater is its cleansing power. In a "Living Water," the water prevents its mineral elements from building molecular connections. This way the elements remain ionized in colloidal form, as a part of the molecule cluster of the water with its geometric pattern, and have no harmful effects on our body. If, on the other hand, the hydrating framework is destroyed by adding carbon to the water, the various elements can unite as inorganic molecular connections.

This scenario is demonstrated by the calcification in our body, in which a combination of calcium and hydrocarbonates is clogging our arteries.

On Drinking Waters

The best water for our health is living, natural, unaltered, mature spring water that is most often low on minerals. It is this kind of water that biophysically has the characteristics of high life-energy: electromagnetic frequencies and vibration patterns that resonate with those in our body. Despite the biophysical quality of water, you should also make sure your natural spring or artesian water is not only low in minerals but also

The best drinking water is pure water which comes from natural springs and is low on minerals

free from pollutants. Nitrate values over 0.03 ounce per 2 pints of water are officially in the safe range and allowed. However, they are not recommended.

In the U.S. alone there are hundreds of brands of bottled waters and as many specialty drinking waters defined and labeled as "artesian," "distilled," "drinking," "mineral," "purified," "sparkling," and "spring" water. Natural waters include spring waters and mineral waters and, as such, must be bottled directly at the source. Unnatural waters include sparkling or carbonated water and most drinking water.

The healthiest waters
are those from artesian
sources, as seen
in the photo

Water without Structure

In the U.S., waters containing at least 250 parts per millions of totally dissolved solids may be labeled as mineral water. For commercial reasons, good quality spring waters are often carbonated. This process extracts the natural hydrogen of the water and adds artificial nitrogen instead. In this way the taste isn't altered, but all germs are destroyed, helping to extend the water's shelf life. But germs, bacteria and fungi can only be found in spring water that has not fully matured or fully developed its crystalline structure. Water needs time to mature and form a crystalline structure. Most spring waters found in supermarkets are immature and are therefore carbonated or ozonated, which destroys the frequency pattern and can be considered as dead, because they have lost most of their information content. Unfortunately the consumer cannot determine whether the water they are buying has been ozonated or left natural, because there is no obligation to declare this information. On the other hand, waters that are not ozonated are not allowed to advertise this fact, due to German laws regarding commercial competition.

Mature, fresh spring water is free of germs and bacteria, due to its crystalline structure

But the quality of drinking waters available at the marketplaces can change and other waters are constantly emerging to replace those currently available. There is an ongoing, lively debate about the health effects of the various mineral waters. Bottled mineral water producers in the U.S. are not allowed to advertise their mineral waters as beneficial for your health. This is not really bad because we have to remember that the body can assimilate only a fraction of these minerals, if at all. If additionally the water is processed, the natural, inherent bioenergetic properties of water, its electromagnetic frequencies and vibration patterns that resonate with those in our body, are altered. The resulting dissonant frequencies in the water have adverse side effects on our body. Drinking such

73

devitalized water that is unable to carry the necessary information in the form of nutrients and vitality to our system, will only create chaos in our body and we will have to suffer the consequences.

Some Facts about Mineral Water

Switching from tap water to mineral water is, in most cases, like jumping out of a frying pan into the fire. Often the quality of local tap water is actually better than that of mineral water from the supermarket. Of course you can drink carbonated water or tap water. Many restaurants don't offer any alternatives to tap water. You should only be aware that neither carbonated water nor chlorinated tap water counts towards the two quarts of water that you should be drinking every day to maintain or achieve optimum health.

Tap water, despite its flaws, is often better than bottled mineral water

---

Facts about Water

Drinking water in the U.S. alone is polluted by up to 300 pesticides and fungicides

The pressure in the water pipes destroys the structure of water.

The minerals in mineral water are too coarse to be absorbed by the body. Therefore, they are of no value for our body and can even be damaging to our health.

It is best to drink natural, pollutant-free, and unaltered water that is low on minerals.

Immature spring waters have not yet built their geometric, crystalline structure and therefore have no value for our health.

Carbonated and ozonated waters are dead waters and have no value for our health.

Nature offers an abundance of beautiful watersheds. However, the best water for our drinking purposes are those coming from natural springs and artesian wells

The Processing of Water

Shocked by headlines such as: "Our Drinking Water is in Danger" or "Death from the Faucet," and fueled by the health and fitness industry, more and more people in the U.S. are looking for alternative solutions to the drinking-water problem. This has created a totally new industry in America: the processing of drinking water. Two types of facilities have been developed: one for biochemical processing, and another for the energetic processing of drinking water. Methods for the biochemical removal of pollutants include active carbon filtration, ionization, reverse osmosis or steam distillation.

Distilled water is
pure, but also
extremely aggressive
and without structure.
Therefore, it is not
recommended for
drinking

Biochemical Processing of Drinking Water

Steam distillation devices remove all chemical pollutants, minerals, and trace elements, leaving H_2O of a purity that can not be found in nature. Therefore, steam distillation creates aggressive water, as the pure H_2O immediately tries to bind itself to all elements. Additionally, the water no longer has structure. With reverse osmosis devices the quality of the water depends on the membrane of the device. The benefit of reverse osmosis is its ability to remove, nearly entirely, any kind of pollutant and the fact that no energy is needed for this process, as it works with water pressure. However, far more water is used for this process than is produced for drinking (with high quality devices the ratio is about 1 to 3). For further information about water processing, turn to the bibliography at the end of this book.

Energizing Water

The market's responses to the demands of those who are aware of "dead water" and are seeking "living water" are: water energizing devices or water resuscitation devices. These devices claim to rebuild the obliterated crystalline structure of the water through a number of exotic methods: by exposing it to the sun's radiation, through magnetization, vitalization, levitation, movement or frequency transmission. These are not chemical but physical processes. Even dead water contains a 4% remnant of living crystalline structure, which is the starting point for the whole revitalization process, in an attempt to make 100% from only 4%. These water-energizing devices, however, claim to do in a few seconds what took nature several hundreds of years. The water does absorb a certain frequency pattern through the energizing process. This is scientifically verifiable. However, these transmitted vibrations are very unstable, so, depending on the device, slight mechanical impacts, such as shaking the water, can cause the loss of the previously restored information. Crucial in this process is the duration for which the water is exposed to the influence of the structuring frequency pattern of the device – the longer, the better. In any case, these devices do not harm the water, and they are better than no treatment at all.

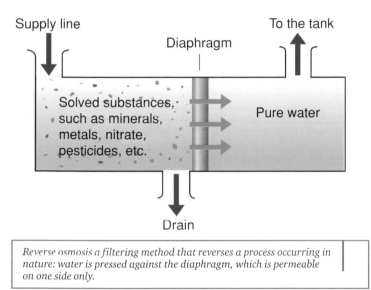

Reverse osmosis a filtering method that reverses a process occurring in nature: water is pressed against the diaphragm, which is permeable on one side only.

Be Cautious with Water Energizing Devices

When buying a water-energizing device, make sure the manufacturer didn't confuse physics with chemistry. Water energizing manufacturers often suggest that their devices make tap water safe for drinking. They claim that the revitalization neutralizes the water's toxins by transforming the negative vibrations into positive vibrations, rendering all the pollutants benign. However, this is not possible with these devices. Any pollutant that is in your tap water will still be there after it flows through such a device because transforming the vibrational frequency of a pollutant means transforming the pollutant itself. The matter making up a pollutant is dependent on the

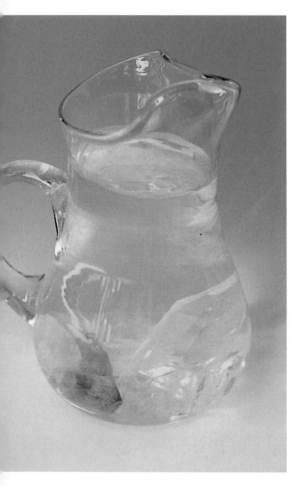

energy responsible for giving it its form. If the pollutant hasn't been transformed and is still present after chemical analysis, then its negative effects have not been transformed either. Physics must not be confused with chemistry. So if you choose to artificially process your tap water, then you should first remove all the toxins chemically, for example with a good reverse osmosis device, and then revitalize it with an energizing device.

Water Revitalization with Quartz Crystals

A natural, very effective and inexpensive method to revitalize your drinking water is to use quartz crystals. Simply place a handful of quartz crystals, such as clear quartz, smoky quartz, rose quartz or amethyst in a glass decanter or jar. In the evening, fill the container with filtered or purified tap water or artesian spring water that you purchased in a bottle. Pour in only as much as you intend to drink the following day and let it sit for at least eight hours.

A mere handful of quartz crystals is sufficient to revitalize our water

Measurements have shown that the surface tension of crystal soaked water reaches values similar to those of water processed by reenergizing devices. The hexagonal structure of the quartz crystals is capable of partially restoring the original, flexible structure of water; this method is applied by many pricey energizing devices that just use simple quartz sand. Crystals cannot remove the toxins from the water, but they can help to transform them and give your water a crystalline and more orderly condition.

Be aware that whatever approach you take to try to make your tap water better, it will never become a genuine, living water such as natural artesian water, where Nature was allowed hundreds of years of time to rejuvenate and recharge it with her energy potentials.

Quartz crystals have the power to restore the original, orderly structure of water

Processing of Tap Water

Water can be processed chemically and/or energetically.

Distillation devices produce the purest water, however they create aggressive H2O whose geometric structure is almost completely destroyed.

Osmosis devices can remove nearly all toxins, but they fail to transform the negative vibration patterns (memory) left from the toxins, and they force the water to surrender all of its crystalline structure.

Energetic revitalization cannot remove toxins.

Quartz crystals reform water's crystalline structure over time.

Ideally, if you choose to drink tap water, you should first remove the toxins with a reverse osmosis device and then revitalize the water by soaking it in crystals for at least eight hours.

Whatever approach you take to improve your tap water, be aware that it will never become a genuine, living water such as natural artesian water, where nature had hundreds of years of time to rejuvenate and recharge it with its energy potentials.

FIJI Natural Artesian Water – The Perfect Natural Therapy

The Fiji Islands are one of the world's last bastions of ecological sanctity

This chapter on water would not be complete without introducing the discovery of one of the most profound water sources in recent years – FIJI Natural Artesian Water. Let us present the whole story to you, so you can discover the fundamental chemical, medical, and biophysical energy potential of this special water, and how we revealed the secrets of a water that is truly blessed with the taste of paradise.

At the center of the macroscopic universe, in solitary isolation, surrounded by thousands of miles of ocean, lies one of the world's last bastions of ecological sanctity the Fiji Islands. They consist of more than 330 islands, each one a real ecological gemstone. The mainland of Viti Levu, with its volcanic highlands and tropical rain forests, represents a one-of-a-kind natural ecosystem. Safe from pollution, pesticides and acid rain, the islands are located some 1,500 miles from the nearest continent and have no polluting industry of their own; one might call these remote Islands as well 'Paradise'. The secret to our precious resources of water is rainfall, which ultimately feeds all natural springs and underground water reservoirs. Some of this rainfall flows into the oceans by forming rivulets, then

streams and rivers. Flora and fauna use some of it up right away. Some of it disappears into the depths of the earth and can remain hidden for decades, even for centuries in underground reservoirs, or aquifers, as they are called.

The proportion of water to land determines the amount of rainfall. So it's not surprising to find the world's greatest amount of rainfall around the Pacific basin, the world's greatest body of water, covering nearly one third of the globe. Converted by and carried aloft on the warming rays of the sun and influenced by solar frequencies, the uncontaminated ocean water vapor around the Fiji Islands, liberated from the salt, are lifted from the ocean upwards through the untainted atmosphere. These vapors condense and return to Earth as pristine raindrops. What happens from here creates the best drinking water of our planet – FIJI Water.

The virgin rainwater, fragile in structure, first needs to be charged within the Earth. Upon falling to earth, it filters through a water-bearing formation of fragmented basalt rock, sandstone and other natural silicates within a 15 km diameter volcanic crater, some 4-5 million years old, located at the Yaqara Valley on the northern side of Viti Levu, then into an aquifer deep beneath the lush volcanic highlands and pristine tropical forests. Influenced by geomagnetic frequencies, this water becomes the "lifeblood" of the Earth. It takes the water decades to reach the underground crater, permeating at an extremely slow rate. FIJI Water naturally contains an amazingly high amount of silica, a most important trace mineral recognized to be vital to our health. Equally important is the finding that this silica is almost completely colloidal. The longer the water is inside the womb of "Mother Earth," the more significantly it will be influenced by the geomagnetic vibrations. Like a battery when fully charged, the water reaches its maximum potential, eventually becoming artesian spring water. Carbon dating revealed this water to be more than 450 years old. Imagine that this water was being collected since a time before the Industrial Revolution, which started only 200 years ago. Enor-

The Yaqara Valley, the source of FIJI Water

82

mous pleasure can be enjoyed from imbibing this unparalleled, natural water, the "lifeblood of the Earth."

In his book "Silica – The Amazing Gel," Dr. Klaus Kaufmann talks about the "Pristine Waters of Fiji." Through repeated lab testing he found that FIJI Water contained the healthiest form of silica, precipitated in natural rainwater from a pollution-free atmosphere. Here, he said, "I was privileged to discover the world's most unique source of precipitated silica suspended in readily absorbable colloidal form. The real boon was to find this silica-rich drinking water in a region free of polluting industry, far from acid rain, nuclear power stations, atomic testing, pesticides, detergents, and other carcinogens that plague so many regions of our planet." This water is also very low in sodium. With a pH level of 7.5, slightly on the alkaline side, the water has a perfect pH level for good health. This gives the water a super soft and refreshing taste, with absolutely no aftertaste.

After hearing of its inherent virtues, FIJI Water founder and owner David Gilmour decided to invest a great deal of personal effort and money in bringing the water to world markets. He had long ago recognized the benefits of natural, and preventative approaches for curbing and treating illness and his research found that the colloidal silica in the water might be an important finding.

David Gilmour had a long history in Fiji prior to the discovery of FIJI water. In 1972, he acquired his private Fijian island of Wakaya. He vowed to keep commercialization away from the shores of his island paradise, and to preserve its natural integrity. One of his great dreams included building the world-famous Wakaya Club resort, where a lucky few can come to savor the island's inherent, unspoiled beauty. David Gilmour was always on the lookout for a source of pure and healthy drinking water. With the discovery of the water source on

David and Jill Gilmour on Wakaya

With a slightly alkaline pH level of 7.5, FIJI Water has a super soft and refreshing taste

Wakaya, where a lucky few may come to savor the unspoiled beauty of this 2,200 acre island, is the fulfillment of one of David Gilmour's life-long dreams

nearby Viti Levu, another lofty dream had come true. Today, there are many educated, health-conscious and active people all over the world who appreciate the purity of his water. "My dream of pure water has come true, just as my dream of Wakaya has. This is a greater discovery than I could have dreamed possible." Inspired by the many benefits of the water, David Gilmour and his company "FIJI Water" have committed themselves to "making a difference." Not only do they support numerous charities throughout the world, but they use the profits from the sales of Fiji Water to support Fijian pre-schools. A trust fund was established for the Fijian people, to give them something in return for their precious water, which they share with all of us. Now that we understand the natural causes for the unique purity of FIJI Water, other important benefits and properties need to be discussed. Medical and biophysical university studies, conducted under double-blind criteria, have revealed astonishing scientific properties of the water. For the results of the recent Univer-

sity studies conducted with FIJI Water, please read the following section "Scientific Results," starting on page 88. The question arises as to why exactly this water is so special in comparison to any other water analyzed? Scientists believe that one
major reason for the unique biophysical properties measured
in the water, which are in resonant reaction to the body, is the
fact that the cluster structure of the water molecules are perfectly organized so as to create an overall information pattern.
From "Healing" and "Holy" water sources in Europe, such as
Lourdes, Fatima, and many more, we have learned that it is not
their chemistry, but rather their biophysical properties, measurable as electro-magnetic field frequencies – the "Life-Force" of
the water – which makes "FIJI" a "Living Water." It is this measurable energy potential that delivers provable health benefits.
The entire planet Earth is enveloped in an energetic grid net,
similar to a spider web, where, at its individual intersecting
points, geomagnetic energy spectrums with unique resonance
levels are detectable. Most interesting is the finding that the
natural spring waters which occur at these specific locations,
called "energetic grid net power points," most often posses
quite measurable energetic frequency potentials. Intense scientific studies, commissioned by the Austrian Government, have
proven that at specific geographic positions, the living organisms of plants, animals and humans, as well as every form of
matter and all of our elements, are directly and immediately
affected in resonance by the energy field of such places. Not
only do the natural spring waters that occur at such locations
hold a vast and unique spectrum of natural electromagnetic
field frequencies. Everything coming into direct, physical pro-
ximity of such places, including the surrounding areas, is affected by its energy field too. Is it a chance that almost all so-called healing waters and precious gold deposits, the metallic
representatives of pure light energy, are found at such grid net

*The biophysical pro-
perties of
FIJI Water make this
water a "Living Water"*

intersections? Maybe the ancient civilisations actually were in possession of this knowledge, and therefore most often build their monumenta, such as pyramids, on energy grids. Later, the Christians chose to build their churches exactly atop these energy points.

This might explain part of the unusually unique biophysical and energetic properties of FIJI Water. The islands of Fiji are geographically situated exactly on the globe where the day starts for all of us. Due to the physics of Geomantic science, the geographical center of the Fijian Islands sits astride one of the energetic power-point locations of the Earth-grid-net. At such intersections of the grid-net, unique energy frequencies can be measured which influence every form of life inhabiting the region. This would explain the unique information pattern analyzed in the FIJI Water, which is absolutely recommended due to its unique chemical composition and purity. But biophysically speaking, it's more than "Living Water," it's a natural, therapeutic treatment with measurable homeopathic properties. To quote Dr. Bruce Shelton, renowned Homeopathic practitioner and President of the Arizona Board of Medical Examiners: "Of all the bottled waters available on the market today, one brand stands head and shoulders above the rest. The brand is FIJI Water. It has the highest content of natural silica without having any harmful contaminants. I drink several bottles of FIJI Water every day and recommend it to all my patients."

The formation of such high colloidal content of silica in FIJI Water makes this water almost equal to the most precious water in our body, our brain fluids. Perfectly ordered in their cluster structure, the brain fluids are almost gelatinous, its fluids containing the highest amount of colloidal silica. We'd like to remind all readers that it is the geometric pattern of matter that creates the energy spectrum. It is the hexagonal structure of silica that makes it possible to store and transmit information in all the world's computers, identical to how our brain functions. This would explain not only the amazing results in skin, bone, nail and hair rejuvenation, but above all the immediate and enormous increase of brain activity due to the continuous drinking of FIJI Water within the university study. Other unexpected "side-effects" that the study revealed included weight loss, better overall concentration, less discomfort associated with menstruation, increased sexual activity, reduced stress, an overall improved outlook on life, and more restful and refreshing sleep.

This almost sounds like a "miracle water." But centuries ago, waters with such amazing healing abilities really were called "miracle waters", because people were unable to understand the reasons for their amazing healing benefits. Today, with modern scientific knowledge, we are able to analyze, measure, and understand the cause of such "miracles." Remember, the healing properties are not the result of chemistry, but of the energy field which creates the "Life Force," and establishes a resonant energy field in all who drink it. The so-called "chemical" elements of the water are the necessary transmitters for what we call the "Life Force." Its energy field, which is bound to the molecule cluster, forms in perfect geometric order. If there was no detectable energy field, nothing would need to be transmitted by the chemicals. It is not the matter or chemical structure that forms the energy field, but it is the energy field that forms the geometric structure of matter to transmit that energy via resonance to our body. Drinking an occasional bottle of FIJI Water may not influence our body significantly. But when FIJI Water is consumed on a continual basis, with a minimum of 1.5 liters per day, then it becomes just a question of time as to when its hidden potency starts to self-regulate our entire organism, empowered and charged by the energy within

> The healing powers are not the result of chemistry, but of the energy field which creates the "Life Force," and establishes a resonant frequency in all who drink it

the water. Even if, for some reasons, you are not able to drink a "Living Water" on a daily basis, as is highly recommended by the authors, then at least use FIJI Water to create your own precious and naturally pure Himalayan crystal salt sole soluti-on to ensure its pristine, essential, inherent benefits.

Scientific Results: Medical and Biophysical University Double-Blind Study

The following section describes the amazing results of a scien-tifically conducted comparison between FIJI water and origi-nal Himalayan Crystal Salt, with its natural living elements, vs. tap water and common industrial table salt. This study will help you to understand the differences in the effects of "Alive" and "Dead" on our body.

Science has discovered the physical and chemical properties of pure FIJI Water and original Himalayan Crystal Salt. Now we take a look at the biophysical aspects of these amazing elements. In conjunction with the Institute for Biophysical Research, the Inter-University Graz, Austria, conducted medical and biophy-sical research using the internationally accepted double-blind criteria for human research. In a double-blind study, neither the researcher nor the subjects are aware of which treatment is received until after the study is completed. This effectively pre-vents any manipulation of the results. The scope of the study was to find out the possible differences in health benefits bet-ween treatments with FIJI Water vs. tap water from the city of Graz, Austria, and FIJI Water with a teaspoon of original Hima-layan Crystal Salt solution, vs. tap water from the city of Graz, Austria with a teaspoon of common, industrial table salt solution. The research scientists and doctors were astonished at their findings. Never before had their test results so quickly and so positively identified a water of such high energy content as FIJI Water.

A Double-Blind-Study means that neither the resear-cher nor the test subjects know what kind of treatment they are getting.

Several individual medical, biophysical and psychological parameters were measured, diagnosed, analyzed, tested and evaluated. Four groups of patients received treatment and diagnoses for a period of nine weeks. All groups of subjects drank 1.5 liters of water on a daily basis. (Group 1: drinking only FIJI Water, Group 2: drinking only tap water, Group 3: drinking a solution of FIJI Water in combination with original Himalayan Crystal Salt, Group 4: drinking a solution of tap water in combination with common table salt). No other treatments were received, and none of the patients used drugs or dieted during the course of the study. The individual subjects of each group had similar conditions to those of each subject of the reference groups (age, sex, weight, health status, etc.). The following section summarizes the results:

At the outset of the study, when analyzing and diagnosing the self-regulatory system of each person through the implementation of the "IMEDIS SYSTEM" (see page 130), the average deviation from perfect health within Group 1 (FIJI Water only), where 0.00 % would be the perfect health status in human organism, was measured as a group index of 30%. By the end of the study, their average group index had positively changed, decreasing towards normal to the level of 9.67%. Moreover, the individual diagnosed parameters of organ functions of the peripherals and nervous system, as well as stomach functions and connective tissue functions, achieved the most significant positive changes. This positive change was highly significant because the opposite was analyzed and measured within Group 2 (tap water only). Their average measured group index at the beginning of the study was 28.80% and was negatively increased to an amount of 40.20% by the end of the study.

Analysis and diagnosis of Group 3 (drinking a solution of natural, original Himalayan Crystal Salt in FIJI Water) showed the

This Double-Blind Study is the most comprehensive and detailed research ever conducted on water and salt

The Double-Blind-
Study shows that
FIJI Water initiates
specific positiv
changes in the
human body

initial average-measured index of 32.3% to drop to an incre-
dible low average index of 8.57% until the end of the treatment. The best results were measured within this group,
whose subjects experienced significant positiv changes in the
respiratory system, the blood circulation system, the skin, and
metabolic system of all organs, including gall bladder, urinary
bladder, and the kidneys. Group 4 (drinking tap water with
common table salt) showed the worst results. The initial average-measured index of 29.20% had risen to 39.39% at the end
of the treatment.

The scientific analysis provided by the IMEDIS System gave
clear medical evidence that persons who, on a daily basis,
drink a minimum of 1.5 liters of FIJI Water only, or as a solution with original Himalayan Crystal Salt, will experience
improvements in the natural regulation of energy deficiencies
in the human organism. The homeostasis (self-regulatory
system) is clearly enhanced and verifiably elevated, so human
bodies react in resonance with the fluids used as a treatment.
Quite the opposite occurs when using tap water and/or common, industrial table salt. This scientifically proved that water
and salt are not just H_2O and NaCl (sodium chloride), but two

of the most important substances for our health and energetic well-being. As an additional biophysical parameter, and in order to analyze the compatibility of the treatment, the medical drug testing device "Voll Electro-Acupuncture System" was employed. It measures skin resistance, so the subjects don't need to ingest any test substances. This bio functional system diagnosis can scientifically prove how helpful a treatment can be for the self-regulatory system of the human organism. Group 1 (FIJI Water only) and Group 3 (FIJI Water combined with Himalayan Crystal Salt) produced the best results. Groups 2 (tap water only) and 4 (tap water with common salt), however, experienced the exact opposite. All tests with patients of Group 1 and Group 3 revealed a positive and resonant feedback, while Group 2 and Group 4 exhibited a dissonant and negative feedback with no compatibility with human organ functions. Because the electromagnetic frequency of FIJI Water is similar to that of the human body, it provides substantial benefits. This "Life Force" could not be detected within the tested substances of tap water and common table salt.

This study was taken one step further by using the highly sensitive HRV system (Heart Rate Variability) together with all

Because FIJI Water has an electromagnetic frequency similar to that of the human body it provides substantial benefits.

Drinking water, whether FIJI Water or tap water, increases the level of "Good Cholesterol" HDL

other analysis methods, to to diagnose possible changes in the biophysical status of the body. For the first time, using the heart frequency rate in combination with typical medical and biophysical analyses within a scientific study under double-blind criteria, significant changes were noted. The clinical group analysis of Group 1 (FIJI Water only) and Group 3 (FIJI Water with original Himalayan Crystal Salt), reflected a significant increased change in the heart frequency in relation to the Sinus-Rhythm. These changes are responsible for an overall increased vitality of all functions of the entire body. The vitality increased on a daily basis during the time when patients were drinking FIJI Water. The opposite results were diagnosed within Group 2 (tap water only), and Group 4 (tap water with common table salt solution). Their vitality decreased.

Blood pressure analysis resulted in no significant changes between Group 1 (FIJI Water only) and Group 2 (tap water only). But within Group 3 (FIJI Water and original Himalayan Crystal Salt Solution), there was a notable decrease in high blood pressure. All patients of all groups were analyzed and diagnosed under medical criteria according to their blood and urine conditions. The Lipoprotein status were first analyzed at the HDL, or

"Good Cholesterol" level, which increased within all tested groups. The level most significantly increased within Group 1 (FIJI Water only) and Group 2 (tap water only), the groups which were drinking only water. University medical research has shown that a high HDL level lowers the risk of arteriosclerosis. Drinking water, be it FIJI Water or plain tap water, increases the HDL, or "Good Cholesterol" level.

The LDL, or "Bad Chlesterol" level, decreased within all four groups. The level most significantly decreased within Group 3 and Group 4, the groups which received the salt solution treatments that were using, in addition to the water, the salt solution treatments. Medical university studies have shown that low LDL levels help against the risk of arteriosclerosis. Independent of the quality of the salt solution, a healthy, low LDL level is maintained by a healthy level of salt in our systems.

The "side effects" included weight loss, noticeable hair and nail growth, increased vitality, and improved power of concentration

The following section will give you an idea of the study's scope. The study included parameters already established for medical research. Psychological and subjective parameters of the patients were established by using internationally accepted questionnaires, such as the Swiss "Basler Well-Being Questionnaire" and the "Pittsburgh Sleep Quality Index." During the course of the nine-week study, a total of 2,260 questionnaires with a total of 51,390 questions were answered by the patients and evaluated by independent university statisticians. In summary, Group 1, drinking FIJI Water alone, had the best sleeping quality and health recovery results. Further, due to the detoxification powers of the natural crystal salt solution, patients who drank the Himalayan Crystal Salt solution made with FIJI Water, felt that their physical, as well as their emotional beings, were being cleansed.

Patients in Group 1 (FIJI Water only) and Group 3 (FIJI Water and original Himalayan Crystal Salt solution) reported that they had more physical energy than before starting the study.

Patients who drank FIJI Water wished to continue drinking the water not only because of the taste but more for the overall feeling of well-being

Some patients reported that this increased energy level helped them to achieve success in their business endeavors. Their brain activity, together with their energy levels during recreational activities and their general vitality, also increased. Some patients in Group 1 and Group 4 reported that they had noticeable hair and nail growth during the study. Almost all patients in these two groups reported an increased ability to concentrate. Overweight patients lost an average of 4 kilograms (approx: 9 pounds) without without any supplements or nutritional diets. Female patients in Group 1 and Group 3 reported that they had less pain during menstruation and almost no depression. One 47-year-old woman, who her whole life had wished to become pregnant, became so during the study when drinking FIJI Water. This may be a coincidence, but patients also reported an increase in sexual activity. Most of all, every single FIJI Water and Original Himalaya Crystal Salt patient reported that it had been a delight to drink FIJI water and take the crystal salt solution. Aside from the positive health benefits they all attested to, there was a certain feeling of enhanced consciousness. After completing the study and treatments, patients who drank FIJI Water wished to continue drinking it, not only because of the taste, but more for the overall feeling of well-being. This desire was not shared by patients in Group 2 (tap water only) and Group 4 (tap water and common table salt).

Never before in the history of the Inter-University of Graz, Austria, had such comprehensive and detailed research been conducted in the fields of water and salt. Due to the huge number of parameters and characterictics of this unique "Water and Salt" study, which employed internationally established double-blind medical criteria, not all significant details could be described within this general summary.

FIJI Natural Artesian Water

The geographical center of the Fijian Islands sits on top of one of the energetic power-point locations of the Earth-grid-net. Influenced by geomagnetic frequencies, this water becomes the "lifeblood" of the Earth.

FIJI Water comes from an aquifer that dates back to a time before the Industrial Revolution. For over 450 years the water has been subjected to the Earth's natural resonant frequencies, developing its full energy potential.

FIJI Water contains the healthiest form of silica, precipitated in natural rainwater from a pollution-free atmosphere.

With a pH level of 7.5, slightly on the alkaline side, the water has a perfect pH level for good health. FIJI Water has a very low calcium and magnesium content which gives the water a super soft and refreshing taste, with absolutely no aftertaste.

FIJI Water and original Himalayan Crystal Salt are both carriers of natural electromagnetic frequencies similar to the electromagnetic frequency spectrum in the human body.

Patients in Group 1 (FIJI Water only) and Group 3 (FIJI Water and original Himalayan Crystal Salt solution), reported that they had more physical energy than before starting the study.

During the study, overweight patients lost an average of 4 kilograms (approx: 9 pounds) without any supplements or nutritional diets.

Never before in the history of the Inter-University of Graz, Austria, had such comprehensive and detailed research been conducted in the fields of water and salt

The

Water&Salt

The Official Magazine of the Water&Salt Association

www.waterandsalt.us

Bi-monthly - bringing you *information*:

- New Scientific Studies
- FAQ's and Letters to the Editor
- Travel Spots and Conscious Dining
- Health, Beauty and Body Care
- Spas, Wellness and Floatation Centers
- New Products
- Recommended Readings
- Nutrition Tips
- Metaphysical Insights

The Magazine for Healthy and Conscious Living

Receive Water&Salt magazine for the annual subscription price of $30 (6 issues) 1st Issue 07/04

Or, visit us online at www.waterandsalt.us and find out about the benefits of membership.

If using a credit card, write name and address as it appears on your statement.

First Name _____ Last Name _____

Address _____

City _____ ST. _____ Zip _____

Phone _____ email _____

- [ ] **Check** (payable to Water and Salt Association)
- [ ] **Credit Card**
- [ ] Visa [ ] MasterCard [ ] American Express [ ] Discovery [ ] Debit Card

Credit Card Number _____

_____ Exp. Date

Signature of cardholder authorizing the transaction

Send to: Water&Salt Association • P.O. Box 190 • Umpqua, OR 97486

Water&Salt

The Official Magazine of the Water&Salt Association

www.waterandsalt.us

Bi-monthly - bringing you *information*:

- New Scientific Studies
- FAQ's and Letters to the Editor
- Travel Spots and Conscious Dining
- Health, Beauty and Body Care
- Spas, Wellness and Floatation Centers
- New Products
- Recommended Readings
- Nutrition Tips
- Metaphysical Insights

The Magazine for Healthy and Conscious Living

Receive Water&Salt magazine for the annual subscription price of $30 (6 issues) 1st Issue 07/04

Or, visit us online at www.waterandsalt.us and find out about the benefits of membership.

If using a credit card, write name and address as it appears on your statement.

First Name   Last Name

Address

City   ST.   Zip

Phone   email

- [ ] **Check** (payable to Water and Salt Association)
- [ ] **Credit Card**
- [ ] Visa   [ ] MasterCard   [ ] American Express   [ ] Discovery   [ ] Debit Card

Credit Card Number

_____   Exp. Date _____

Signature of cardholder authorizing the transaction

Send to: Water&Salt Association • P.O. Box 190 • Umpqua, OR 97486

Salt

The White Gold of Earth

Salt has the same fundamental importance to our life as water. We could not survive without water or salt. Salt is as vital as water. All the properties of salt that relate to our body are closely connected to water, because the crucial properties of salt – biochemically as well as biophysically – only exist in combination with water. The crystalline *sole* (so-lay), the saltwater brine, is unquestionably the energy matrix in which life begins, develops and subsists.

When in the following chapter we scrutinize the properties of salt, we mean salt in its original form: holistic, wholesome, unaltered, natural salt, as it has crystallized in the Earth over millions of years. When we speak of "table" salt that is sold in the supermarket, we refer to it as sodium chloride with additives, which is what it really is.

Salt is equally important for our body as is water

Water and Salt – Two Equal Partners

If water is reputed to be our number one food source, then salt is certainly our second main source of food. Accordingly, from our experience, we will treat both elements equally, because none of us could live without either. Interestingly, an abundance of literature can be found on the biophysics of water. Sadly, little is known about the biophysics of salt, as it has managed to escape closer scientific investigation. We would like to close that gap with this chapter, and we hope that there will be other scientists coming forth to undertake research on this intensely interesting subject.

Crystal salt runs in glistening clear, pink, and reddish veins through the salt mountain

Water and Salt – Primary Building Blocks of Life

Upon close examination we find that the human body is made primarily of water and salt. Natural crystal salt contains all the elements of which the human body is comprised. From the periodic table of elements we are familiar with 94 natural elements (stable as well as unstable). Apart from inert gases, all of these elements can be found in crystal salt. Hence, crystal salt contains all natural minerals and trace elements that are found in the human body.

We perceive crystal salt as being the totality of all natural elements. This may not be entirely correct according to chemistry, however we will continue to use the term crystal salt in this context. The number of the respective elements contained in the crystal salt is biophysically irrelevant to this study.

Vitamins and proteins are neither found in water nor in salt. However, when we analyze water and salt in the body, we find that vitamins and proteins are nothing but partially complicated molecular chain links of elements, which we can find individually within the salt as well as in the body.

Water, salt and light, as energy forms, can construct highly geometrically structured chain links which are – biochemically – identical to vitamins and proteins. This is what gives the *sole* such a significance as a life-builder, and makes it well worth taking a closer look at.

> Crystal salt contains all the minerals and trace elements of which the body is made

Salt — Mediator between Energy and Matter

Salt is what remains after matter has dissolved and transformed into subtle matter. The founder of the Schüssler Salt Therapy, Dr. Wilhelm Schüssler, more than 100 years ago had already proved that the ashes remaining after a corpse is cremated are nothing but the salts of which the human body is made. A by-

product of the modern waste burning plants is salt. Needless to say, no one would want to eat this salt, but nevertheless it is salt. Our prehistoric ancestors were already aware of the vital necessity of salt. Wherever they found salt they guarded that location like a treasure. Later in history, salt was called "white gold" and became the subject of political power plays, which often resulted in war. Roman soldiers were actually paid with salt, which is reflected in the word "salary." Salt was more important for survival than gold. All over Europe, salt routes emerged on which the "white gold" was transported. The names of many German cities bear testimony to this time, with names as, Salzgitter, Salzburg, or Salzuflen, for instance. Also, names including the word "hall," the Celtic word for salt, emerged, with city names like Bad Reichenhall, Friedrichshall and Hallein, indicating salt deposits at these locations.

Water and salt, in combination with light, can even build proteins

The Meaning of the Word "Salt"

The word "salt" comes from the Latin term sal, which again comes from the word sol. Sol is synonymous with the "*sole*," the

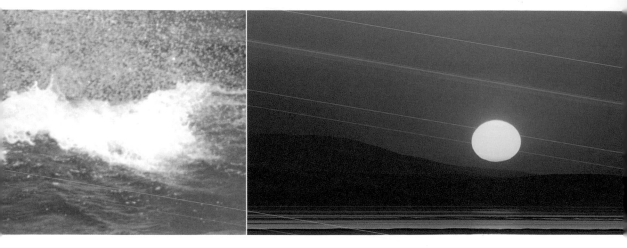

water and salt solution, and is the Latin word for sun. Mythologically, and from its definition, *sole* means "liquid sunlight", i.e. liquid light energy, bound into a geometrical structure, capable of creating and sustaining life. This literally explains where life on Earth came from: from the *sole* of the primal oceans.

The Celtic word for salt, "hall" has the same roots as the German word "heilig", meaning "holy". Furthermore, hall signifies sound (German schall). The schall is a sound with a long hall, which means echo or reverberation in German, involving vibration. If we knew of these correlations today, we would be asking our neighbor at the table to "Please pass me some vibration," rather than "Please pass me some salt." Were the Celts aware of the fact that salt contained all the frequency patterns of the elements? And did they know that "hall" was the basic vibration for "heil" (German "health")/"wholesomeness"? They definitely knew how to cure illnesses and rebalance the energy deficit in the body through "hall," their salt. From an energetic as well as from the biophysical point of view, an energy deficit can be

Salt used to be more valuable than gold and was used as a form of payment balanced with salt, regardless of the missing frequency pattern, or the missing information/energy/life-force. Pure crystal salt is still geologically defined as "halite," in which we can recognize the Celtic words "hall" for salt and "lit" for light. Loosely translated, crystal salt or halite means "light vibration.

The Structure of Salt

Similar to water, salt has a specific crystalline structure. In contrast to the structure of water, which is tetrahedral in shape, the grid structure of salt is cubic in form. This cube is constructed from light quanta, also called photons, which are pure light

The Meaning of Water and Salt for Life

Water and salt are the building blocks for the creation of life.

The human body consists of the two elements: water and salt.

All complex molecular chain-link connections, such as vitamins and proteins, can be produced with sole and   sunlight.

The ash left over from the cremation of a corpse is pure salt.

The word salt is based on the Latin word sole for sun, and the Celtic word hall. Hall represents the root for the German words heil and schall, which mean "wholeness"/ "wholesomeness" and "sound vibration"/"reverberation".

The Celtic word hall also means the same as the German word "seele", or soul in english. The Celts believed that the soul originated from the ocean, the sole.

energy The light/heat energy of the sun evaporated the primal oceans more than 250 million years ago and the energy expended for this dehydration is stored in the platonic body of the salt's crystalline grid as potential energy. By adding water, the force of the grid can be overcome, so that the energy it holds is liberated. In this process, the elements within the crystal salt are ionized, allowing them to penetrate the body's cells. This creates an ocean of energy, a powerful potential, just waiting to create and sustain life.

The meaning of the Celtic word "halite" is "light vibration"

The crystalline grid of salt consists mostly of

◯ = Sodium

◓ = Chloride

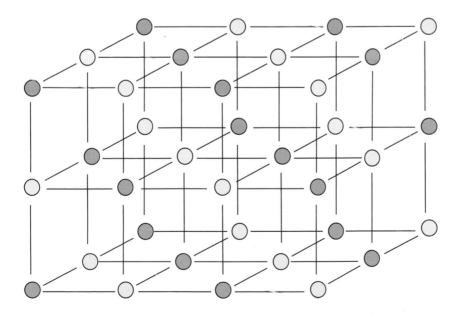

The Mutability of Salt

From a scientific point of view, salt has a very unique property. In contrast to all other crystalline structures, the atomic structure of salt is not molecular, but electrical. This fact is what makes salt so mutable. When we submerge a quartz crystal into water and remove it after 10 minutes, it is still the same quartz crystal. It did not change molecularly, though it has a crystalline structure. Although the crystal can give its energy, its frequency pattern into the surrounding water, which is effortlessly absorbed, the quartz crystal remains the same. The crystal is too rooted in matter to be dissolved or disassociated from its polarity.

When we submerge a crystal of salt into water, it dissolves, and the *sole* is created. *Sole* is neither water nor salt. It is a higher energetic dimension than either the water or the salt alone. When the *sole* evaporates, the salt is left behind. This transformability of salt ensures that it does not have to be metabolized in our body. Starch is transformed into sugar, protein into amino acids and fat into glycerin and acid – but salt remains salt. It is directly available to the cells in its ionized form as *sole*. All other foods must be separated into their components in order for the body to make use of them. But salt always remains in its original form. As *sole*, it even accesses our brain directly.

No Thoughts and No Actions Without Salt

Even the most simple process in our body needs salt or its inherent elements in ionized form. For example, it is the task of our nervous system to transmit to our brain the stimulation that has been recorded via sensory input. The brain in return passes this information back to our muscles in order for us to react. An electric potential occurs at the membrane wall of the cells when the positively charged potassium ions leave the cells and the positively charged sodium ions cannot enter due to their size. The outside becomes positively charged and the inside negati-

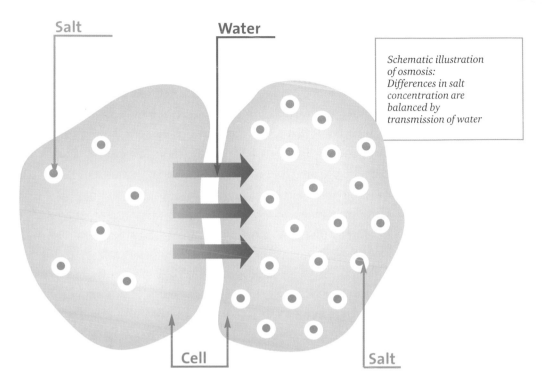

Salt

Water

Schematic illustration of osmosis: Differences in salt concentration are balanced by transmission of water

Cell

Salt

Osmosis, the Principal of Metabolism

The mutability of salt is very important for our body because it is the foundation of our cell metabolism. The life-giving principle of metabolism in all living beings is osmosis, when liquids transfer from one cell to another.

This process of osmosis is controlled by the salt concentration in the cells. The liquid in a cell always moves from a cell with a lower salt concentration (potential) to a cell with a higher salt concentration (potential), because the cell membranes are permeable for water but not for salt, and the body always strives to achieve a balance in concentration.

Without the
elements potassium
and sodium found in
salt, we could neither
think nor act

vely charged. When a nerve cell is stimulated, its membrane suddenly becomes polar opposite and consequently is permeable for the sodium ions. In one-thousandth of a second (1/1000th), the electrical potential is transformed and releases, with every nerve impulse, 90 mill volts of energy. The received stimuli are now being converted into thoughts and actions. Without the elements potassium and sodium in the salt, this process is not possible.

Not even a single thought is possible, let alone an action, without their presence. Just the simple act of drinking a glass of water requires millions of instructions that come as impulses. In the beginning there is the thought. This thought is nothing but an electromagnetic frequency. The salt is responsible for creating this frequency and transmitting the command to the executing muscles and organs.

The Conductivity of Salt

From science class, most of us are familiar with an experiment on the conductivity of salt. We attach two ends of an interrupted electric circuit to a light bulb and submerge it into a glass with distilled water. Because this water is not conductive, the bulb does not light up. But when we add a little bit of salt into the water, the bulb instantly begins to glow. It is the same with our body. If we lack the natural elements of the salt, we are suffering from a chronic loss, a chronic energy deficit, or deficit of information. Salt cannot be labeled as a medication, because that would imply that apples were a medication, too. Salt is a core essential nutrient with exceptional abilities and qualities fundamental for keeping us alive. In natural crystal salt we can find what our body might be lacking: the respective frequency pattern, as well as the necessary bio-chemical availability.

There is a perfect example of how a lack of energy can cause suffering. At times we hear of major electrical shutdowns where several states and millions of people are affected. Everyone in those areas suffers from this lack of energy.

Now isn't this also an example of something lacking? But in this example it reflects a lack in our society. Something is missing in our society that needs to be replaced. Only then can we restore balance and come into perfect harmony. We have to understand, through suffering, what exactly we have to add to our lives. Here, our society is also a body suffering. If we choose, we can look for the cause and eliminate it, just as we look for the cause of our own individual suffering. In this way, we can eliminate the suffering of all of society, bringing the whole world into perfect balance and peace.

Salt can balance an energy deficit

The Extraordinary Qualities of Salt

Its crystalline structure is electric, not molecular.

Due to its mutability, salt does not have to be metabolized by our body in order to be absorbed.

Osmosis, the foundation of cellular metabolism, is controlled by salt.

Without salt we could neither think nor act.

Crystal salt in both its original form and in granulated form

White Gold To White Poison

Our blood is a 1% sole solution, equal to the salt concentration of the primordial oceans

As common as salt shakers are to our kitchens, so are the numbers of diseases associated with salt's daily use. Life is not possible without salt. But our consumption of salt is killing us. Why is that? Because our regular table salt no longer has anything in common with the original crystal salt of which we're talking about here. Nowadays, salt is mainly sodium chloride and not salt. Natural crystal salt consists not only of two, but of all natural elements. These are identical to the elements of which our bodies have been built, and from which life was formed in the primordial oceans.

Interesting enough, our blood is a *sole*, containing the same salty solution as that of the primal sea; that is, a fluid consisting of water and salt. It also has the same ratio of concentration as existed in the days when life left the primal sea. Driven by the forces of gravity and levity, this *sole* flows through more than 56,000 miles of waterways and blood vessels throughout our organism, and regulates and balances the functions of our body.

How Salt Became Sodium Chloride

With the advent of industrial development, natural salt was "chemically cleaned" and reduced to the combination of sodium and chloride. Essential minerals and trace elements were removed as impurities. However, sodium chloride is an unnatural, isolated, unwholesome substance having nothing in common with salt. Similar to white, refined sugar, salt, once regarded as white gold, was converted into white poison. However, there is a higher reason for salt having been endowed with all the natural elements found in our bodies. Sodium chloride is an aggressive substance which is perpetually seeking a biochemically equalizing counterpart, so that the body's pH can always remain neutral. Sodium chloride needs its natural counterpart in order for it to produce its effect. The natural counterparts, such as potassium, calcium, magnesium and other minerals and trace elements, feature, from a biophysical standpoint, specific frequency patterns. These patterns ensure the geometric structures in our body. If these structures are missing, we are lifeless and without energy. Salt should not be used to add flavor to our food, but for its vibration pattern, which is similar to our body!

Table salt has nothing in common with natural salt

How Table Salt Burdens the Body

While our body only requires a minute amount of 0.007 ounces of salt per day, most of us suffer from a lack of salt, even though we're over-saturated with sodium chloride. When our consumption of salt is less than 0.007 ounces per day, salt craving kicks in. The average daily consumption of table salt per capita in the U.S. is between 0.4 ounces and 0.7 ounces. However, our body is only able to excrete 0.17 ounces to 0.25 ounces a day through our kidneys, depending on our age, constitution and sex. The body recognizes table salt as an aggressive cellular poison, an unnatural substance, and wants to eliminate it as quickly as possible in order to protect itself. This causes a constant over-burden on our organs of excretion. In almost every preserved product, salt was used as part of the preservation process. So, by adding salt to this already salted food, the body receives more salt than it can get rid of.

The body now tries to isolate the overdose of salt. In this process, water molecules surround and neutralize the sodium chloride by ionizing it into sodium and chloride. For this process, the body must use its most perfectly structured cell water. The respective body cells are dehydrated and die.

The Consequences of Consuming Table Salt

The result of consuming common table salt is the formation of overly acidic edema, or excess fluid in the body tissue, which is also the cause of cellulite. That's why doctors tell us to avoid salt. For every .035 ounces of sodium chloride that cannot be eliminated, the body needs 23 times this amount of its own cell-water to neutralize the salt. If the sodium chloride is still too high, re-crystallization of the table salt occurs as the body uses available non-degradable animal proteins (as those found in milk), which also have no value and cannot be broken down and eliminated. The body uses these proteins to produce uric acid in order to get rid of the excess salt. As the body cannot dispose of uric acid, it binds itself with the sodium chloride to form new crystals that are deposited directly in the bones and joints. This is the cause of different kinds of rheumatism such as arthritis, gout, and kidney and gall bladder stones. This re-crystallization is the body's makeshift solution for the cells and organs in order to protect the body from irreparable damage caused by an irresponsible diet. But in the long run, it poisons the system because those substances cannot be disposed of.

The Power of the Chemical Industry

In view of these facts, we may ask why natural salt, so vital for our life, is chemically processed and turned into poison for our consumption. The motive is rather simple: About ninety-three percent (93%) of the worldwide salt production is more or less directly used for industrial purposes. And for this, pure sodium chloride is required. Also, every chemical process requires pure sodium chloride. The remaining, natural elements, are considered impurities and discarded as unwanted. The chemical industry has made use of the unique interrelated forces of salt for innumerable processes and products which have enabled industrial progress. Sodium chloride is essential for soda, laundry detergent, varnish, plastic, PVC – nearly everything that distances us further from nature on a daily basis. Six to seven percent of the salt production is used in the food industry for inexpensive preservation purposes. There is hardly a single ready-made or fast-food product which doesn't contain sodium chloride, be it yogurt, bread or ham. This has been a blessing to the logistics of the food industry, because now they are able to extend the shelf life of many of their products for up to one year. However, for the human body, this has been a fatal development.

93% of the world's salt production is more or less used for industrial purposes and another 6% is used as food preservatives

The Salt in our Kitchen

Only an insignificantly small amount of the worldwide salt production ends up in our kitchens as "salt," here commonly referred to as table salt. By intense advertising campaigns, the salt industry tries to convince the general public of the health advantage of halogens in salt, such as the highly toxic iodine (in form of iodide compound). Fluoride is another popular additive to table salt, an extremely reactive, greenish-yellowish, piercingly sharp gas with stinging odor that also belongs to the group of halogens. Both are artificially added – iodine claiming to be of benefit to the thyroid, and fluoride allegedly to strenghten our teeth. However, both components only add to the perils of sodium chloride.

The questionable and refutable hypothesis that Germany is a country which lacks iodine, has caused not only the entire country of Germany, but also Switzerland and Austria to be indirectly and forcefully medicated with iodine. This commercial campaign started in Germany in 1995 and has been one of the most successful propaganda campaigns of the last ten years. So it comes as no surprise that the majority of the German general public believes that the artificially "iodine-enriched" table salt is actually healthy for them, and therefore are willing to consume it. However, the scientific insights on adding iodine and fluoride to sodium chloride must be critically examined. More people are suffering from the consequences of these substances than are claimed to be helped by them. The body is simply not capable of metabolizing artificially provided iodine and fluoride compounds. Amongst scientists, it is already known that nitrates belong to the most aggressive carcinogenic substances and breed selective cancer in numerous organs. Food additives such as iodine, fluoride, thiozynate, chlorogen acid and metal salts have an accelerating effect on the production of nitrates in the stomach. Iodine is first on the list of substances that cataly-

Additives such as iodine and fluoride increase the aggressiveness of salt

Pure crystal salt will maintain its natural pinkish color even when finely granulated

ze and accelerate the production of nitrates, by literally six-fold. One important consideration for cancer prevention is to completely avoid iodine. Japan, one of the countries with the highest iodine deposits in the world, also has a 25% rate of thyroid cancer. In other countries the thyroid cancer rate decreases proportionally to the decrease of iodine consumption. Less iodine means less cancer. Even the renowned German magazine Öko-Test" (Eco-test) labelled halogen compounds from such halogens as iodine, fluoride, bromine and chloride as inappropriate for consumption, because most of these compounds cause allergies and are carcinogenic. A U.S. study found that adding iodine to salt could be the cause of a decrease in male sperm cells. Furthermore, most table salt contains preservatives, which are not mandatory to be indicated. These include calcium carbonate, magnesium carbonate, as well as aluminium hydroxide, to prevent the grains of salt from clumping together. Aluminum is a light metal that is known to accumulate in the brain. It is assumed that the high rate of Alzheimer's disease in the U.S. is linked to a high consumption of preprocessed foods packed in aluminum, as well as to a high consumption of soft drinks from aluminum cans. The distress caused by aluminum prevents the bridging of nervous pathways, which blocks our thought process. After all, it is the natural salt, containing all natural elements of the Earth, removed as impurities by biochemists, that enables our brain processes to even function. Salt consisting of all the natural elements is, mistakenly, regarded by the biochemical industry as being contaminated. In reality, only the naturally occurring calcium, potassium and magnesium found in salt can be absorbed and used by the body. We need salt in its holistic form, with all the natural elements, in order for our bodies to function perfectly. We need calcium, potassium and magnesium in the exact proportion and order as they appear in natural salt in order for our body to absorb and optimally utilize these minerals and trace elements. We need salt in its holistic state, with all its inherent natural elements, so that our body can function the way it is designed to.

The Differences Between Natural Salt and Common Table Salt

Our blood is a sole, identical to the primal ocean.

Table salt consists of sodium, chloride and additives and has nothing to do with real, natural, holistic salt.

Table salt is a dangerous cellular poison that the body tries to eliminate or store, at an enormous expense of energy and effort.

Natural salt is crucial for maintaining vital functions in the body.

Head Natural Salt Deposits

Salt is plentiful on Earth, especially in the oceans, which cover approximately 70% of the surface. However, the oceans are being degraded to waste-disposal-dumping facilities and are being polluted with heavy metals like, lead, cadmium, arsenic, mercury, and more. Not a single year passes without headlines about at least one fractured tanker causing a major ecological catastrophe. Of course, the poison elements also have their own vibration patterns which are dissonant and therefore harmful to our bodies. For these reasons, sea salt nowadays doesn't have the same positive impact on our health as it used to. In addition, 80% of all sea salt producers are refining their salt. But there is still sufficient pure, holistic salt available on Earth, left when millions of years ago the sun evaporated the primal oceans. This crystal salt that exists within mountains is still as pure as the ancient primal oceans and contains all the elements as found in our body. Such a crystalline *sole* is a vast source of energy.

Rock Salt

Salt deposits, as found in salt mines, consist of 95% rock salt. Since rock salt is a wholesome, natural substance, it is far more valuable than table salt. Biochemically, it is non-aggressive.

However, the elements within the rock salt have not undergone sufficient compression to be fully fused into a crystalline grid or lattice of structured order, but are only attached to the surface and along the fissures of the rock salt. This means that, even though all or most of the natural elements on Earth are found in rock salt, they are too coarse and unrefined to be absorbed into our cells. Because salt is not a molecular compound in its solid state as a crystal grid, the elements sodium and chloride are in an ionized colloidal state, as are all the other elements, suspended and fully integrated within the crystal grid. The valency of the elements depends on whether they have been subject to sufficient compression over millions of years, which integrated them into a crystal grid.

The Difference Between Rock Salt and Crystal Salt

The elements in rock salt are not integrated into the salt's crystal grid, but cling to the outside surface and crevices of the crystalline structure. This is the fundamental difference between rock salt and crystal salt. A salt crystal manifests a superior structure. Due to this sublime form, the elements are biochemically available for our cells, as are the individual frequencies or vibration patterns. Rock salt is a cheap alternative to table salt, and is at least a natural and wholesome product. Biochemically and biophysically however, it is of little importance to our organism. We can only receive the resonant effects of the geometrical structure through the superior order or structure of a crystal and our cells can only absorb those elements that occur in an ional form. Only under considerable pressure can the elements be transformed into a specific size, making them ional, so they can pass through our cell wall. This is important because our cells can only absorb what is available organically or ionally. Therefore, we cannot absorb the minerals from mineral water as they're not refined enough to penetrate our cell walls. And

The minerals in rock salt are too coarse to enter our cells

what doesn't get into our cells cannot be metabolized. Therefore, the best calcium is useless if it is not available for the body's cells. In order to make any use of an element, we need its organic, or ional, state, in perfect natural symbiosis with all associated components.

Crystal Salt

Pure, natural crystal salt has been subjected to enormous pressure over millions of years. The pressure is responsible for creating the salt crystals. The higher the amount of pressure the more superior or excellent the state of order within the crystalline structure. Salt, for us, is foremost an information carrier and not a spice. For information to be absorbed into our cells, a crystalline structure is necessary. Chemically, a stone and a quartz crystal are both silicates. However, they are distinguished from each other by the amount of pressure they were subjected to. The quartz crystal embodies a perfect geometric form, a perfect state of order within its structure. The stone does not. Its elements are coarse, because it was not subjected to enough pressure to create a crystalline structure. Crystal salt layers wind through the mountain of salt, shimmering in transparent white, pinkish or reddish veins. Only by sufficient pressure could the salt inside the salt mountain be transformed into crystal salt.

The elements trapped within the crystal occur as particles, small enough to be able to penetrate the human cells and be metabolized.

Mining Crystal Salt

Crystal salt in its most perfect form is geologically referred to as halite. In olden days it was called "king's salt" because its use was a privilege reserved for nobility. The populous received mere rock salt. Crystal salt mining was abandoned a long time ago, when it ceased being profitable. Because pure crystal salt only occurs sporadically and in veins, it cannot be mined and processed mechanically. Often it is necessary to mine one hundred times the amount of rock salt in order to secure the precious crystal salt. Biophysically, crystal salt must be mined manually in order to retain the natural qualities of its frequency spectrum. However, the manual mining of salt is economically unrealistic. In order for people to experience the potential and the regenerating effects we have discovered in crystal salt, it is necessary to make it available. Holistic theories are significant only when they can be put into practice and proven. So when we talk about all the natural elements being present in crystal salt and have comprehended how essential this substance is for our body, the next step is to make it available for proving. Not all salts found in crystal form have similar qualities. Just because rock salt assumes a crystalline form doesn't mean that it is of the superior quality that we are talking about.

The minerals in crystal salt are available in such small particles that they can be easily absorbed by the cells

Researching Crystal Salt

To date, scientific interest in the biophysical qualities of salt has been slight. This is the reason for so little research having been done so far in respect to the qualities of the salt elaborated upon in this book. Scientific probing and analyzing of crystal salt, in the forbidding depths of the salt mine, is both extensive and extravagant. Up to now it was neither of any interest to the salt miners nor to the general public. Only after the publishing of research data, gathered from the analytical study of crystal salt that was mined in Berchtesgaden, Germany, and in the Himalayan Mountains in Pakistan, did public and scientific interest soar. Unfortunately, the release of this data also encouraged the introduction of fraudulent or "knock-off" crystal salt into the marketplace, and companies are just using the name as a brand identity, the quality of which one should be aware and cautious.

When purchasing
crystal salt, be sure
to check its origin
and proof of quality

This is especially true for so-called "crystal salts," coming from places as Northern Germany, Poland and the salt plains of central Pakistan, regions not having the geological prerequisites to form crystal salt. Or when so, they have not been subject to any degree of biophysical analysis to learn of their possible benefits. The salt from these areas are mostly crystalline rock salt or at best, a mixture of rock salt and crystal salt, due to the fact that the separation process was careless and machine managed. Oftentimes, pink shimmering rock salt is sold as "crystal salt" because, to the inexperienced eye, it cannot be identified by its appearance.

Although a variety of "crystal salts" will become available following the release of this book, some displaying almost equal chemical composition, offered by companies trying to convince you

Crystal Salt from the Himalayan Mountains

The scientific insights about crystal salt published in this book refer to one specific salt, mined from only one exclusive location in the Himalayan Mountains. The scientific research conducted by Peter Ferreira in this book, refers only to this salt, which in English-Speaking countries is distributed as "Original Himalayan Crystal Salt," and meets the criteria for scientifically verifiable holism. It was only this pure crystal salt that was used to conduct our research. The degree of compression within this mountain range was so extreme that it created perfectly structured crystal grids within the salt.

The salt bears the official seal of the Royal family to denote its region of origin. This seal symbolizes the longevity and the holistic, natural lifestyle of the native people of this region. We are proud to have been granted permission to exclusively identify the original Himalayan Crystal Salt, which is the foundation of this book, with this seal. Initially, we also analyzed crystal salt from a German mine in Berchtesgaden. The chemical analysis only slightly varies between this salt and the crystal salt from the Himalayan Mountains in Pakistan. However, the Original Himalayan Crystal Salt exhibited a structure that was substantially more perfect, more orderly and hence contains that much more information.

The distribution of the elements also plays an important role. According to the global table salt regulation (Codex Alimentarus), consumer salt must consist of at least 97% sodium chloride. Even though this guideline has nothing to do with holistic nutrition, or in fact with any nutrition at all, it has to be observed in order to sell salt as food. This industrial standardization enabled the import of refined table salt while disabling salt mines to sell their natural rock salt as food, because the sum of natural elements within the rock salt surpassed the legal limit of the codex. However, the Himalayan salt we have been researching also satisfies the codex because of the extraordinary compression of its elements. It is not a question of the number of elements, but about how they are qualitatively available to the cells in our body. This structure of superior quality has been scientifically proven in the "Original Himalayan Crystal Salt."

that it is of the same standard as we are talking about here in the book, it must be understood that natural salts from different sources also possess different biophysical properties. Remember how fascinated you were when first seeing the individual structures, reflecting the energy potentials of the various water crystal photos from Emoto? Although it was only H_2O, we could clearly see that its individuality was totally dependent on its

This label is your guarantee that you have the Original Himalayan Crystal Salt as talked about in this book

energy field. For salt and all other elements, the same biophysical science is enforced. This doesn't mean that the original Himalayan crystal salt we have tested and used in our studies is the "best" salt available, because in biophysics there is no "best" or "worst." Every source is dependent on its measurable, individual energy frequency spectrum and, therefore, not comparable. But to know for certain how beneficial a "crystal salt" can be for us, we need to seriously analyze it thoroughly. These studies take a considerable investment in both time and money. Only then, after having conducted the research, you can really know about its true benefits in respect to our physical and mental well-being. Additionally, we would like to remind the reader that this book is, in general, about the subject of biophysics. And, that the holistic and biochemical perspectives are shown to you only so that you can see that all things existing, even the "invisible" ones, are connected to each other. When Peter Ferreira made his first physical and biophysical measurements to prove his thesis that salt is more than its chemical composition, he made his initial testing with patients in the healing chambers of the salt works in Berchtesgaden, Germany. This underground salt universe, which is the most famous salt mine in Germany, is at the center of the intersections of energetic grids of the Earth. Just by understanding the neutral physical properties of salt in general, Peter Ferreira has proven that, even without ingesting any salt, the patients' energy fields were immediately affected in resonance to the physical energy frequency spectrum present where this salt occurs. Tests performed on patients two hours after having left the salt chamber revealed that their positively changed organ and cell status had maintained the same energy level as while in the salt mine. Knowing that not everybody has the opportunity to visit such healing chambers as the salt works, Peter Ferreira started to analyze the effects of drinking a teaspoon of pure, crystal salt solution from this mine. Amazingly, patients who never were physically at the salt mine adopted the resonant energy field spectrum of the mine and maintained it for more than 24 hours. This encouraged patients to use the crystal salt solution as an every-day treatment until their self-regulatory systems could start to regenerate. After years of testing, Peter Ferreira started to use rare crystal salts from places in the Himalayan Mountains, known energetic points on the Earth grid net. That is the reason why the "Crystal Salt," in biophysical terms, became so valuable in connection with the "Living Water" for creating the "*Sole*". The *sole* releases its stored energy potential, in relationship to its source, into our entire physical being, whereas our entire body reacts in resonance with the desire to regenerate to its healthy, complete origin, by enhancing our consciousness level with the given information pattern. Therefore, thousands of patients were able to completely recover from serious health defects by understanding these simple, natural rules. But again, even though it appears to be a "miracle," it is just the natural and universal law of "Cause and Effect."When thinking about health, don't make it complicated. Nature is easy to understand. Just allow yourself an open mind to understand what "Life" really is.

The aim of our studies was to prove the so-called "invisible", to make our readers aware that reality is more than just what we see and touch, and to show what is the invisible force behind the creation of what we call matter – our "Life Force"!

> The crystal salt releases its stored energy potential, in relationship to its source, into our entire physical being

What You Should be Aware of When Purchasing Crystal Salt

Naturally, in order to preserve the inherent vibration pattern within the Original Himalayan Crystal Salt, it must be hand-mined. This increases not only its value, but consequently its price, too. Expect to pay more for this salt than for other table salts, sea salts or rock salt. Therefore, be mindful of the quality

of the product you intend to buy. Be critical, and ask the merchant where they get their salt from, which region and which salt mine. Also ask for the required analysis of the crystal salt. Request the verification of the presence of all the natural elements and of their availability to the cells. Investigate as to whether the salt fulfills the Codex Alimentarius, and make sure it was manually hand-mined and prepared. You really have to be critical, due to the unfortunate fact that a number of "crystal salt" merchants have emerged with their eyes on profits rather than on our health. They are hawking common rock salt or inferior salt from mines in Poland, the salt plains of Pakistan and elsewhere, bearing the label of high quality, Himalayan crystal salt. It would be regretful if some commercially minded exploiters, only seeking their profits, would discredit such an important discovery as the utilization of precious water and salt for maintaining our health. The original Himalayan crystal salt from the Himalayan Mountains that was used for conducting the medical research revealed in this book continues to be utilized by the medical profession and possesses all named essentials and fulfills all requirements. Today there are several hundred doctors and therapists utilizing this ancient holistic knowledge. For thousands of years, doctors have successfully treated their patients with nothing more than water and salt!

For more information, please contact the independent Water&Salt Association, whose address you will find in the Resources section at the back of this book. In the appendix you will also find a list of addresses for further information about the Original Himalayan Crystal Salt and other resources.

More and more people are discovering salt as a vital source of life

Healthy Energy Management with Water and Salt

Surely there are other deposits of crystal salt in the world and our planet has an abundance of it. Industrialization may have supplanted this ancient knowledge, but it's time to revive this know-how and rediscover crystal salt as a vital food source. You will be surprised how quickly you can regain your body's natural energy balance. There are many health-conscious individuals who shop at health and natural food stores. However, many are simply nonchalant in regard to the most important foods, water and salt. One study showed that subjects who were less health food conscious, but consumed water and salt of highest quality, for the most part had healthier organs than health conscious people who paid no attention to the quality of the water and salt they were consuming. You should understand that you can become physically and mentally independent if you choose to drink natural, artesian, living spring water and you choose to eat pure crystal salt, instead of table salt. However, this is not about just regaining your total health. We're also talking about balancing and managing your energy, which can be maintained by the information bound in the water and the salt. These two elements contain everything to satisfy your body and your mind.

Biophysically, water and salt, when combined, give you everything your body and mind needs

Water and Salt as Real Foods

This combination of water and salt, this natural crystalline *sole*, is not a wonder drug. Rather, it's simply a living food source. Water and salt can reestablish order from chaos in your body. However, you must first realize the cause of this chaos and remove it for long-term beneficial effects. In many cases, a change of diet is necessary. Crystal salt also releases the toxins and superfluous waste products in your body that can then be transported and excreted by your system.

The Healing Effects of Salt

Many people are irresistibly drawn to the ocean because, instinctively, we want to return to our origin

For thousands of years salt has been known as a panacea. Alchemists called it "the fifth element" – besides water, earth, air and fire – because its qualities were comparable only to ether, the actual fifth element. Why are we so drawn to the ocean? Because our subconscious mind instinctively wants to return to the specific vibrational state of the ocean from which we once emerged. This is where we can return to recharge our batteries and regenerate. It was only about 200 years ago, with theadvent of industrialization, that we initiated our disconnection from nature and her ways. Fortunately, we are witnessing a trend to return back to natural, holistic methods for living and caring for our body, including a shift back to utilizing natural salts in this process. People everywhere are reconsidering the healing effects of natural crystal salt. We can find it in skin care lotions and for use as bath salts, and it is even used in inhalation or cleansing treatments for illnesses of the respiratory system and for a variety of other indications.

The Neutralizing Effect of Salt

The healing properties of salt are also known in allopathic medicine. The largest and oldest salt works in Europe occupies the royal salt mine of Wieliczka, Poland, just 7.5 miles off Kra kow. Here, a hospital was carved out of the expansive salt mountain, 740 feet below the surface, specifically for asthmatics and patients with lung disease and allergies. Several thousand patients have been successfully treated in this hospital. The healing rate is astonishingly over 90%. Recognition of the healing effects of salt chambers has influenced the construction of a similar underground spa located in the salt mine of Berchtesgaden in Germany. The therapeutic benefits of long-term residency inside the healing salt chambers are allopathically acknowledged. The healing effects were originally thought to be related to the purity of the air within the mine's chambers. But if it was only a question of the purity of the air, why was the air in the cave so healthy, and the air above the surface so unhealthy? One cause has been determined. Our houses are charged with electromagnetic devices, such as TVs, stereos, computers, microwave ovens and the basic electric currents running through our walls. And, when not at home, we hold cell phones to our ears while driving in our cars and walking through our daily lives. This electro-smog causes an excess of positively charged ions that disturb the balance between the positively and negatively charged particles. Further, it creates an excess of positively charged, chemically unbound particles in the air. Only thirty seconds on a cell phone are enough to open up our blood-brain-barrier, a natural barrier that protects our brain from toxins, for eight hours. A Swedish study showed that ninety percent of the women who used a copper-T I.U.D. as their birth control method, while simultaneously using cell phones, developed uterine cancer; the cause being that the T.I.U.D. acted as a transmitter and receiver of unnatural, dissonant vibrations.

Harmful radiation for the body– the cell phone

Salt Caves and Chambers —Natural Hospitals

Salt has the natural ability to balance the positive charge. In olden times it was customary for farmers to cover newly constructed rooms with salt before they moved in, in an attempt to chase away evil spirits. The evil spirits of yesteryear are today's dissonant electromagnetic vibrations. But the neutralizing force of natural salt can balance the detrimental frequencies of electro-smog. This special characteristic of salt is utilized by the atomic industry where, in the abandoned salt chambers of Gorleben, they store spent atomic fuel cylinders. The salt can neutralize radioactive radiation.

The healing effects of the salt chambers are not just caused by the purity of the air, but primarily by its resonant vibrational pattern

It is not just the purity of the air in the salt chambers that has such healing effects, but more so its resonant vibrations, that activate our self-healing and self-regulating powers. When our body is sick and lacking its natural frequency, salt can bring us back into our original, balanced state. Deep in the heart of the Earth, surrounded by millions of tons of salt, patients can encounter the influence of the enormous power of the salt's balancing frequency or vibration, thereby replenishing the body and balancing its energy deficit. In principle, all symptoms of illness can be therapeutically neutralized through salt. A remarkable study done on patients with liver disease has proven this phenomenon. After two and a half hours in the salt cave, their liver conditions improved drastically. Obviously, the liver patients could not be healed in such a brief period of time, because their illness had already manifested within the physical organ. Unless the healing salt chamber therapy was repeated on a daily basis, the patients would relapse to their original state of vibration twenty-four hours after leaving the salt chamber. On an energetic level, however, as long as the patients remained in the healing salt chamber they maintained a healthy state. An alternative to a lengthy stay in a salt chamber is the crystalline *sole* drinking therapy, as has been tried and proven hundreds of years ago.

The Healing Power of Salt

The healing effects of salt are based on its specific frequency vibration that balances the body's energy deficit.

The neutralizing forces of salt can cancel out or negate harmful electromagnetic vibrations in our environment.

Allopathic medicine is also familiar with the healing effects of salt and implements it especially with respiratory ailments and skin diseases.

Research Findings

Many of the research findings in this book regarding water and salt are based on numerous studies conducted over the past few years. The knowledge acquired about the biophysical and biochemical qualities of water has been verified through many scientific studies. The scientific community also recognizes the significance of salt for the human organism. However, analysis of the natural holistic properties of salt, as well as of its biophysical qualities, was lacking. In order to close this important gap, the Institute of Biophysical Research has implemented an extensive study under the guidance of Peter Ferreira, to analyze the biophysical effects of salt on the human organism. Renowned scientists, physicians and researchers have also contributed in confirming the importance of using natural water and salt therapeutically. The crucial difference between common table salt and crystal salt is not so much in its biochemical composition, but rather in its biophysical effects on living creatures. For measuring these effects, several biophysical examination methods are available, e.g. the electroacupuncture according to Dr. Voll, the segmentary diagnostics or the organometry with the IMEDIS system, both derived therefrom, and the biophoton analysis with the green alga Acetabularia acetabulum.

Biophysical Examination through Segmentary Diagnostics (IMEDIS)

The expert system IMEDIS captures the primary state of homeostasis as well as the immediate reaction of the body to altered environmental influences. In diagnosing the body's reactions to one or several environmental influences, the patients were subjected to a so-called "neutral" environment. The result of these referential measurements serves as a comparative basis for measurements of bodily functions within altered situations. These measurements were performed according to the procedure of biofunctional organometry, as well as to the methods of segmentary diagnostics. The focus of this test was to pinpoint the energetic and informational effects on the homeostasis (biofunctional regulatory behavior) of the human organism.

The results of the organometric measurements confirm, without ambiguity, its supportive effects through a continuous decrease in deviating factors. The diagnosis of the organs and the reactions in the vegetative nervous system illuminates the energetic and informational relationship between the water and the crystalline *sole* from Himalajan Salt, and its effects on the homeostatic regulatory behavior. This diagnosis helps determine the major pathological and pre-pathological tendencies as well as functional disorders and physiological tensions.

Research Study with Crystal Salt and Table Salt

Let us also take a look at the difference in the results of drinking a regular table salt solution and drinking a *sole* solution made from original Himalayan crystal salt. The body's direct and indirect reactions to the various applications of salt can be seen in the graphics on the front cover of this book. The illustrations on the folder in the front cover show the segmentary diagnosis of the dysfunctions of the organs and the sympathetic nervous system. Illustrations 1 and 2 show the original state of the subject. Illustrations 3 and 4 show the subject's reactions to drinking a table salt solution, illustrations 5 and 6 after drinking the Himalayan crystal salt solution. Initially, the subjects were all given one teaspoon of table salt solution. The illustration clearly shows how the existing dysfunctions of the organs and the nervous system further increase and how an energy deficit is created through the consumption of table salt. This is due to the fact that the body has to draw on its own energy resources to neutralize the unnatural, aggressive substance and eliminate it. Within one hour of drinking one teaspoon of table salt solution the subjects were given one teaspoon of original Himalayan crystal salt solution/*sole*. The diagnosis that resulted from this test not only clearly shows how the energy deficit is counterbalanced, but further, how the original dysfunctional states of the organs and the nervous system have begun to regain balance (see illustration 5 and 6). The examinations have been examined during a time span of 2 hours and clearly illustrate the immediate effects of the table salt in a negative way, as well as of the Crystal salt in a positive way. For illustrations on the IMEDIS Study, see folder inside front cover.

Research Studies with 400 Volunteers

Test Procedure

In order to verify the scientific insights regarding salt, nearly 400 volunteer patients were diagnosed within the framework of this research study. Of those, 197 were continually monitored. The original goal of the study was to examine the effects of specific water and salt therapies on the human organism.

All of the volunteers were asked to drink the daily amount of half a gallon of biophysically precious, natural spring water in combination with one teaspoon of natural crystalline *sole* made from original Himalayan crystal salt. The volunteers where asked not to consume any kind of refined salts and use only the crushed crystal salt for seasoning their foods. Those under continuous monitoring were examined on a monthly basis. All others were only sporadically examined. The foundation of the study required strict adherence to the therapy over a period of three months. The eating habits of one group were intentionally not altered because this might have lead to incorrect conclusions. The effects of water and salt on the body were biophysically examined.

Test Results
The tests confirmed that all of the previously determined organ dysfunctions regained their original, natural state of balance, thereby proving the regulating and balancing power of the crystalline *sole*. These results, gained by Peter Ferreira and showing a positive effect of Himalajan Crystal salt on the human organism, were recently confirmed biophysically as well as medicinically through a Double-Blind-Study conducted at the University of Graz, Austria.

The Measurement of Biophotons in Green Algae (Acetabularia acetabulum)

Living cells emit light. This fact was first discovered in 1922 by Prof. of Med.. Alexandar Gurwitch and rediscovered and clearly proven with the most modern methods of research by German Professor of Biophysics, Fritz Albert Popp. It was also Prof. Popp who created the term, "biophotons" for the light within cells. Since that time, many researchers confirmed that cells in all living beings emit a ultra weak light which increases when a cell is damaged or in the process of dying and ceases to exist with the death of the cell. Scientists agree that the measurable light of a cell is the expression of an energy field that is inherent in each cell and is controlling and regulating the life process.

In our testing, the light emission of the single cell algae give information about the energetic state and about the influence of agencies (crystal salt or common table salt). The Acetabularia Algae can only survive in saltwater and therefore die quickly in fresh water.

Test Procedure

The measurements have been made with the Photomultiplier PMS 3 at the International Institute for Biophysics in Neuss, under the supervision of Professor Fritz Albert Popp.

There was a series of glass kuvettes (10x10x25mm) into which an individual cell of green Acetabularia acetabulum was placed and filled with 100ml of distilled water. (Photo A) The samples were put in the Photomultiplier PMS 3, and measured. The samples were stimulated with a white-light xenon lamp. The time lag of the light emission, delayed luminescence of the algae (Photo B), was measured by the PMS 3 and the data were recorded by a computer. In total, the measurements took 10 hours, in our case, 585 minutes, during which time the Acetabularia samples were stimulated 40 times. Each salt solution and respective control were tested three times.

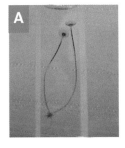

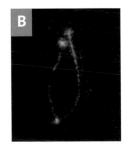

Test Results

The Acetabularia acetabulum algae naturally inhabit saltwater and, when put into freshwater, they die slowly. However, the higher the mineral content of the fresh water, the slower is the process of death. Drastic changes occur with the presence of other substances or by alteration of the solution. The biophotonic emission of the algae tells us about its ability to survive in the tested water, an accurate method for rating water quality. (freshwater quality)

Interpretation

If a biological system is stimulated by light, it stores this light and releases it with a delay factor (delayed luminescence). The first factor of this delayed luminescence, NB-1 Factor, is an important factor. It sheds light on the ability of a system to provide energy and was used, in this case, to interpret the results. To make the data we acquired from the individual algae comparable, we established a baseline. With this baseline all the subsequent NB-1 factors were divided by the first NB-1 result of the respective algae. For the evaluation we took the average of three measurements per test and displayed it graphically.

The Fresh Water Graph (black)

The freshwater test was chosen as the control. Due to the different osmotic pressure the cell is absorbing water until it bursts and quickly dies. The short-lived amplified light emission is typical of a cells struggle with death.

The Table Salt Graph (gray)

Despite the identical 1% concentration between the liquid in the cell of the algae and the surrounding salt solution, the cell dies in a solution made with table salt. However, the death process takes longer than with the freshwater experiment.

The Crystal Salt Graph (red)

In the chosen Original Himalayan Crystal Salt, 1% crystal salt solution, the algae survive. The difference between table salt and crystal salt for the algae is startling and striking. Death vs. Life!

Obviously, the result of this experiment, like any experiment, cannot be completely applied to a human organism, but it shows clearly how delicate living organisms react to various salt qualities. Besides the NaCl (sodium chloride) content, we assume that there are other factors inherent in the salt which play an important role for life. More research is necessary to get to the bottom of this phenomena.

The nominated NB-1 numbers of the test are presented in the following graphic.

Graphic Portrayal of the Experiment with Acetabularia Acetabulum Algae

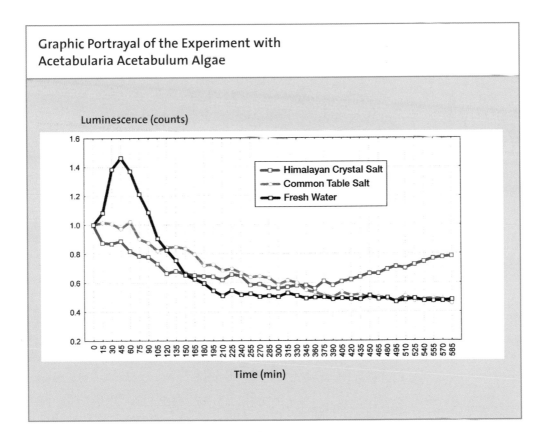

Luminescence (counts)

Himalayan Crystal Salt
Common Table Salt
Fresh Water

Time (min)

Testing Vinegar with Table Salt and Crystal Salt

You can make this test at home with vinegar. Take two glasses and add one inch of vinegar to each. Then, in one glass, add two tablespoons of regular table salt and the same amount of fine crushed Himalayan crystal salt into the other glass. You will see how the regular table salt will start to foam, (depending on the substitutes used in refining), emitting aggressive chemical gases and how the crystal salt will sink to the bottom and dissolve without any reaction. The reactions in your body are similar. Just as with the vinegar and table salt, your body must sacrifice its own precious energy to neutralize the salt. Which effect would you prefer?

Crystal Salt Promotes the Excretion of Animal Proteins

A further study showed some interesting allopathic results. All subjects in this study drank one-teaspoon of *sole* daily. After four weeks, the protein emission in the urine significantly increased for eighty percent of the one-hundred-twenty-three subjects. This shows that the energy pattern of the *sole* with its innate, natural antagonism towards the proteins, helps and supports the excretion of animal proteins that are difficult to break down. (This examination was done by Dr. med.. Elisabeth Scherwitz-Josenhans.)

Quality Analysis of Himalayan Crystal Salt, Sea Salt and Table Salt

Another study, performed by Dr. Wilhelm Höfer, focused on comparing regular table salt with sea salt and original Himalayan crystal salt. Thin layer films of crystallized colloidal suspensions from both the solid and dissolved states of the three distinct kinds of salts were examined. The photographs shown here were taken from this test and are reproducible at any time.

Picture A shows the characteristic crysta struc- ture of the origi-

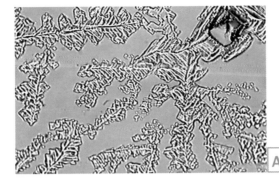

A — Crystal salt
400x magnification

nal Himalayan crystal salt, at 400x magnification. This picture shows a holistic, delicate, living structure, an excellent food source. All elements are interactively combined in an ional state. The crystalline structure is constantly morphing, never static, and hence, never undivided. Pictures B and C show how the dead minerals in the table salt and sea salt take on a state of static isolation. Furthermore, you can see in Picture A how the spaces between the crystalline branches are completely empty, which verifies that this salt is completely free of any kind of dead or polluted substances, such as radioactivity, electro-smog or pesticides. This crystal is full of life! When taken as food, it will have a vital energetic effect on the body. The result is only a net gain in life-generating power for the body, with zero energy loss.

B — Common Table salt
400x magnification

Picture B shows that refined, common table salt has no living crystals. The decomposition during the refining process tore the crystalline components from their framework, their natural symbiosis, and isolated them. To integrate this substance back into a living organism, such as our body, would require enormous amounts of energy to try to revitalize it at the sacrifice of our own precious cell liquid. You can see how the crystals of table salt are rectangular, which gives them no power of their own to stimulate a living organism. In contrary, the organism must use its own life-force to partially metabolize it.

C — Sea salt
400x magnification

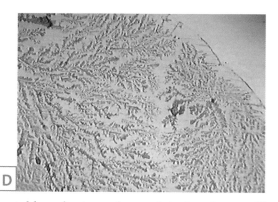

The result is a damaging loss for the body and zero net again.

Picture C shows sea salt to be a combination of crystal salt and table salt, irregular and isolated crystalline structures disconnected from the natural elements surrounding them. Because of this, the body cannot absorb the vital minerals, however many it may contain, unless the body expends tremendous energy to vitalize them. This will also deplete our body of its precious energy. The net gain is negligible with an even greater loss of energy.

Picture D, of original Himalayan crystal salt 100x magnified, displays delicate branching, exhibiting its vitality. The even crystalline structure reflects the salt's harmonious effects. Pictures E and F show table and sea salt 100x magnified. Picture G exhibits how there are no rough edges, densities or shadows in the delicate branch structure of the crystal salt. Which means that the energetic conditions are balanced. By using this salt in our food as a seasoning, its effects will not be inorganic and sclerotic but stimulating and enlivening. To compare: Pictures H and I show table and sea salt 40x magnified.

The results confirm that crystal salt contains powerful life building forces for the organs and the nervous system. The photos also show how unsuitable table salt is for consumption. Sea salt assumes a medial role. It's not as detrimental as table salt, but an ional-colloidal integration of its elements will never be possible.

Crystal salt
100x magnification

Table salt
100x magnification

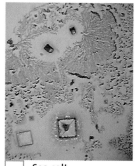

Sea salt
100x magnification

Dr. Höfer's analysis is confirmed by the scientific photography made by the "Institute of Scientific Photography" in Germany, called "Institute für wissenschaftliche Fotografie". Thanks to Prof. Manfred Kage, using light microscopy as well as raster electron microscopy, the differences between the salts could be visually supported. We can witness the crystal salt's flowing formation in Picture K, which indicates how this salt is in resonance with its environment. The salt in Picture L, in com-

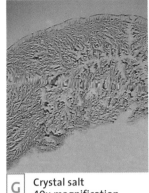

G | Crystal salt
40x magnification

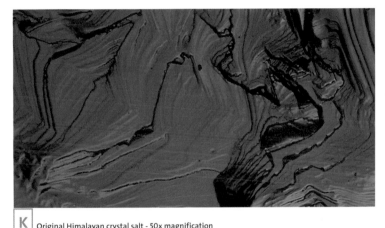

K | Original Himalayan crystal salt - 50x magnification

H | Table salt
40x magnification

L | Table salt from the Himalayan Mountains - 50x magnification

I | Sea salt
40x magnification

parison, shows its unnatural, isolated structures, void of life, resembling the re-crystallized salt deposits in our body. The structural energy patterns of the Himalayan crystal salt also become visible in Ruth Kubler's photography of drops. She has dedicated her art to visualizing geometry and has been able to make the information content within a crystalline structure transparent. These pictures speak for themselves.

(Picture M and N)

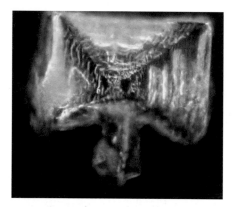

 Photo of a drop of water saturated with original Himalayan crystal salt

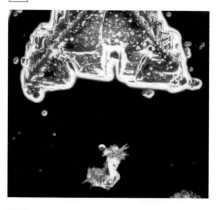

N Photo of a drop of sea water from Antarctica

Certificate of the Analysis of the Original Himalayan Crystal Salt Institute of Biophysical Research, Las Vegas, Nevada, USA

June 2001

Originally, the intention was to include all the elements up to Order Number 90 into the chemical and physical analysis. Following the elaborate analysis of the crystal salt from October 17 2000, the Order Number of the elements was increased to 94 in the frequency spectrum test. All natural stable and unstable isotopes were considered. However, artificial and unstable isotopes were not included for consideration.

Element		Order Number	Results	Analysis Type
HYDROGEN	H	1	0.30 G/KG	DIN
LITHIUM	LI	3	0.40 G/KG	AAS
BERYLLIUM	BE	4	◄0.01 PPM	AAS
BORON	B	5	◄0.001 PPM	FSK
CARBON	C	6	◄0.001 PPM	FSK
NITROGEN	N	7	0.024 PPM	ICG
OXYGEN	O	8	1.20 G/KG	DIN
FLUORIDE	F-	9	◄0.1 G/KG	POTENTIOMETER
SODIUM	NA+	11	382.61 G/KG	FSM
MAGNESIUM	MG	12	0.16 G/KG	AAS
ALUMINUM	AL	13	0.661 PPM	AAS
SILICON	SI	14	◄0.1 G/KG	AAS
PHOSPHORUS	P	15	◄0.10 PPM	ICG
SULFUR	S	16	12.4 G/KG	TXRF
CHLORIDE	CL-	17	590.93 G/KG	GRAVIMETRIE
POTASSIUM	K+	19	3.5 G/KG	FSM
CALCIUM	CA	20	4.05 G/KG	TITRATION
SCANDIUM	SC	21	◄0.0001 PPM	FSK
TITANIUM	TI	22	◄0.001 PPM	FSK
VANADIUM	V	23	0.06 PPM	AAS
CHROMIUM	CR	24	0.05 PPM	AAS
MANGANESE	MN	25	0.27 PPM	AAS
IRON	FE	26	38.9 PPM	AAS
COBALT	CO	27	0.60 PPM	AAS
NICKEL	NI	28	0.13 PPM	AAS
COPPER	CU	29	0.56 PPM	AAS
ZINC	ZN	30	2.38 PPM	AAS

Element		Order Number	Results	Analysis Type
GALLIUM	GA	31	◂0.001 PPM	FSK
GERMANIUM	GE	32	◂0.001 PPM	FSK
ARSENIC	AS	33	◂0.01 PPM	AAS
SELENIUM	SE	34	0.05 PPM	AAS
BROMINE	BR	35	2.1 PPM	TXRF
RUBIDIUM	RB	37	0.04 PPM	AAS
STRONTIUM	SR	38	0.014 G/KG	AAS
YTTERBIUM	Y	39	◂0.001 PPM	FSK
ZIRCONIUM	ZR	40	0.001 PPM	FSK
NIOBIUM	NB	41	◂0.001 PPM	FSK
MOLYBDENUM	MO	42	0.01 PPM	AAS
TECHNETIUM	TC	43 UNSTABLE ARTIFICIAL ISOTOPE - NOT INCLUDED		
RUTHENIUM	RU	44	◂0.001 PPM	FSK
RHODIUM	RH	45	◂0.001 PPM	FSK
PALLADIUM	PD	46	◂0.001 PPM	FSK
SILVER	AG	47	0.031 PPM	AAS
CADMIUM	CD	48	◂0.01 PPM	AAS
INDIUM	IN	49	◂0.001 PPM	FSK
TIN	SN	50	◂0.01 PPM	AAS
ANTIMONY	SB	51	◂0.01 PPM	AAS
TELLURIUM	TE	52	◂0.001 PPM	FSK
IODINE	I	53	◂0.1 G/KG	POTENTIOMETRIE
CESIUM	CS	55	◂0.001 PPM	FSK
BARIUM	BA	56	1.96 PPM	AAS/TXR
LANTHAN	LA	57	◂0.001 PPM	FSK
CERIUM	CE	58	◂0.001 PPM	FSK
PRASEODYNIUM	PR	59	◂0.001 PPM	FSK
NEODYMIUM	ND	60	◂0.001 PPM	FSK
PROMETHIUM	PM	61 UNSTABLE ARTIFICIAL ISOTOPE - NOT INCLUDED		
SAMARIUM	SM	62	◂0.001 PPM	FSK
EUROPIUM	EU	63	◂3.0 PPM	TXRF
GADOLINIUM	GD	64	◂0.001 PPM	FSK
TERBIUM	TB	65	◂0.001 PPM	FSK
DYSPROSIUM	DY	66	◂4.0 PPM	TXRF
HOLMIUM	HO	67	◂0.001 PPM	FSK
ERBIUM	ER	68	◂0.001 PPM	FSK
THULIUM	TM	69	◂0.001 PPM	FSK
Ytterbium	Yb	70	<0.001 ppm	FSK

Element	Order Number		Results	Analysis Type	
Lutetium	Lu	71	<0.001 ppm	FSK	
Hafnium	Hf	72	<0.001 ppm	FSK	
Tantalum	Ta	73	1.1 ppm	TXRF	
Wolfram	W	74	<0.001 ppm	FSK	
Rhenium	Re	75	<2.5 ppm	TXRF	
Osmium	Os	76	<0.001 ppm	FSK	
Iridium	Ir	77	<2.0 ppm	TXRF	
Platinum	Pt	78	0.47 ppm	TXRF	
Gold	Au	79	<1.0 ppm	TXRF	
Mercury	Hg	80	<0.03 ppm	AAS	
Thallium	Ti	81	0.06 ppm	AAS	
Lead	Pb	82	0.10 ppm	AAS	
Bismuth	Bi	83	<0.10 ppm	AAS	
Polonium	Po	84	<0.001 ppm	FSK	
Astat	At	85	<0.001 ppm	FSK	
Francium	Fr	87	<1.0 ppm	TXRF	
Radium	Ra	88	<0.001 ppm	FSK	
Actinium	Ac	89	<0.001 ppm	FSK	
Thorium	Th	90	<0.001 ppm	FSK	
Protactinium	Pa	91	<0.001 ppm	FSK	
Uranium	U	92	<0.001 ppm	FSK	
Neptunium	Np	93	<0.001 ppm	FSK	
Plutonium	Pu	94	<0.001 ppm	FSK	

Additional Combined Elements				
Water	H2O	1.5 g/kg	DIN	
Ammonium	NH4+	0.010 ppm	Photometrie	
Nitrate	NO3-	0.09 ppm	Photometrie	
Phosphate	PO4 3-	<0.10 ppm	ICG	
Hydrogencarbonate	HCO3-	<1.0 g/kg	Titration	

The inert gasses Helium- He-2, Neon-Ne-10, Argon-Ar-18, Krypton-Kr-36, Xenon-Xe-54, and Radon-Rn-86 could not be included in the research. Many of the elements could not be proven with conventional chemical analysis. Through the transfer of frequency patterns by means of wave transference, it was possible to prove the frequency pattern with the aid of frequency spectroscopy. With this, the detection of elements even smaller than <0.001 ppm was proven. The research analysis confirmed the holistic properties of the original Himalayan crystal salt. The sodium-chloride content is 97.41% and meets the worldwide necessary standards for table salt.

g/kg– Grams per kilogram DIN– German Institute for Standardization
ICG– Ionchromatography   AAS– Atom absorption spectrometry
TXRF– Total reflection-XRay-
   Florescence-Spectrometryppm– Parts per million
FSM– Flamespectrometry   FSK– Frequency Spectroscopy

The

Sole

Symbiosis of the Life-Force

At this point our understanding of the two elements of water and salt should have expanded within our consciousness, taking us to a higher level, allowing us to look at this topic from a completely new perspective. All life-giving processes in our universe, from the macrocosm to the microcosm, are closely interlinked to the energy potentials that are released when water merges with salt. These diamagnetic energies that are released by the combination of salt and water, act implosively (temperature decreasing) according to nature's blueprint. The blend of water and salt, the so-called *sole*, is the "mother soup" of all life forms and a flexible, physical representation of pure sun and light energy. The word *sole* is derived from the Latin word for sun "sol", as it is the liquid materialization of sunlight. *Sole* means "liquid sunlight" or "liquid light energy."

Sole is the "primordial soup," the source of all life

Sole – An Ocean of Energy

When water and salt connect, the negative poles of the water molecules surround the positive ions in the salt, and the negative ions in the salt are surrounded by the positive polarized particles of the water molecules. This changes the geometric structure of the water and the salt, and creates something entirely new, a third dimension. The water is no longer water and the salt no longer salt. The elements have liberated themselves from their restrictions, given up their polarities by the resonant

effects, and reached a higher form of energy. Only through this process of attaining higher levels of consciousness can we relinquish our polarities and return into the oneness of all elements. This is exactly what transpires when water and salt meet. In return, the willingness of the water to give up its own identity liberates the salt from it material bounds, overcomes the powers of the gridwork and separates sodium from chloride. Both elements are ionized, which releases their stored

On the Intelligence of Atoms and Humans

The further we break down matter into its components, the more potent its frequency spectrum becomes–physically speaking. As the nucleus measures a higher frequency spectrum than the atom itself, the element within a molecule again measures a higher frequency spectrum than the molecule itself, the molecule higher than the the cell, the cell higher than the organ, and so forth.
In this case, energy, as information, is equal to intelligence, which means that the individual atom is far more intelligent than the matter it creates, and the individual cell is more intelligent than the organ it builds.

The human, made of the sum of all elements, cells and organs, is less intelligent than his individual components. This could explain why our organs consist of a self-protecting system which guards them against poor nutrition. The following scale of vibrational frequencies, will support this premise:

Nucleus $\qquad$ 1022 Hertz

Atom-Element $\qquad$ 1015 Hertz

Molecule $\qquad$ 109 Hertz

Cell $\qquad$ 103 Hertz

Organ $\qquad$ 102 Hertz

Human (Body) $\qquad$ 8 to 10 Hertz

This scale shows that a single water molecule has far more intelligence than a human being. And the degree of intelligence of one individual person is again higher than that of the state or nation of which he is a citizen. This might explain why some of the federal laws are incomprehensible to individuals.

energy and information. The same effect could be achieved without water in the smelting process, extracting metal from ore, and would require a temperature of 1,500° F.

The Creation of Life

It took Earth three to four billion years to create life through the interplay of sunlight, water and salt. Most of us have forgotten that we come from the ocean. But when we look at a sperm cell, we see that it consists of 99% water and 1% salt. Looking from this perspective, a sperm cell is just like a drop of the "mother ocean". The American chemist Stanley Miller proved that all creation began in the ocean. He showed how electric charges, placed in a *sole*, started to collect amino acids and combine organic matter. Although fascinating, it's not completely accurate to say that life was created out of practically nothing. In fact, life is created out of everything, or better still, the "all" that is, because the natural crystalline sole contains all elements that exist on Earth. Our body consists of the same

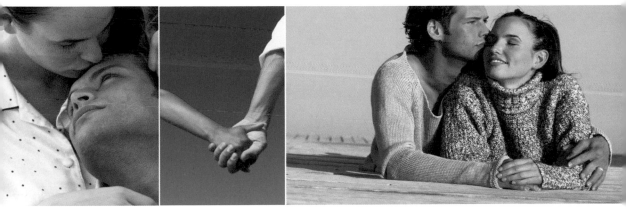

elements as water and salt. Even the ratio of concentration in our blood is the same as that of the primal ocean.

Begetting a Human Life – The Marri-Age of Humanity

The creation of *sole* from water and salt resembles the procreation of a human life. Just as the water and the salt are willing to sacrifice their own identity in order to reach a higher form of being, new life arises out of the merging of two polarities – the sperm and the egg. The ultimate expression of self-sacrifice is when the sperm and the egg unite, becoming one, in order to create something new, a genuine act of unconditional love, the highest potential force of our creation.

Chemists refer to this process, when different elements of the same frequency and polarity merge together, as "molecular-marri-age." Interestingly, the German word for marriage is "Hochzeit" which literally means "high time," the most precious time of one's entire life, when new life is made. Although the English word "marriage" has a slightly different meaning, we can arrive at the same conclusion regarding the definition.

The first part of the word, "Marri," comes from the Latin word "mare" – the ocean – the marriage of water and salt – from which all life originated. Also, in the Bible, we use the mythological term of "Mary" the mother of "Christ," whereas "Mare" means the ocean – the *sole* – where everything had its beginning. So "Marri-Age" basically means this "Golden Age" when "Marri"-"Mare"-"Mary"-"Merry," come together and enjoy *sole* – " Consciousness" – at its highest, most valuable potential – when polarities overcome their existence and new life (a child) is created. This creates a resonant effect. Not only is the energy contained, but it also increases exponentially to a new dimension – new life comes into being. In our realm we refer to this procedure as "marriage." If our individual polarities are willing, within this marriage, to sacrifice themselves for a higher form of consciousness, then our energies increase exponentially with implosive effects to a higher dimension of consciousness. Following the inner ethical principal, it's not only about sustaining life, but also about creating new life.

Achieving "All"-Consciousness

Our innate sexual energies attract each other like magnets. The desire to experience this "merry age," marriage, is deeply rooted within us. Both polarities are striving to combine with each other and resonate, according to the mathematical laws of "plus" and "minus," supported by electromagnetic attraction. We follow our intuitive wisdom and are willing to step into a higher dimension of experience outside of our polarity, through unconditional love. Step by step, the mental wavelengths of the building energies between the two polarities are slowly transferred to our physical rhythm. The male giving-force will tenderly merge with the female receiving-force. Liberated from our polarities, we penetrate the realms of consciousness and for a moment, we experience the highest

When two people get along, they share a common wavelength

feelings of joy, free from space and time. We refer to this experience as an emotional, as well as a physical, orgasm. Our energies pour out and flow unconditionally. In this brief moment we experience divine unity and attain a state of all-consciousness. Through the act of unconditional love, two polarities with the same wavelength have perfectly complemented each other. Neither has sacrificed themselves for the other, but both have sacrificed part of themselves for the goal of consciousness.

Overcoming Polarity

Some people, however, are so deeply caught in their polarities, that they have difficulties in relating to the recently mentioned "merry age" among humans, much more in actually experiencing

Water is the humblest of elements.
It is soft and we cannot grab hold
of it in our hand, yet it can dissolve
the hardest stone

it. And many experience the building forces of sexual attraction in a destructive manner. Instead of raising these energies to higher dimensions of consciousness, most people waste their highest potential energy because they're not able to liberate themselves from the material manifestation of their polarity. The animal instincts outweigh the divine virtues. Tired and exhausted, having drained their own energies, they must first recuperate in order to repeat this destructive process over and over, according to an unconscious instinct. In the wake of this depletion of consciousness they like to blame others for their condition. They're constantly trying to judge between good and bad, according to polarity. They only look at the outer circumstances of their existence and begin to fight.

We are accustomed to supporting one or another cause within the realms of polarity. Power-plays, both at work and at home, erode our strength and drain our energy. We desire to fight diseases without noticing that each time we fight against something, it is senseless, because resistance automatically creates-counter resistance. Still we justify our struggle, because we think we are noble in fighting against that which is negative. Following our polarity, we take sides, which wastes our energy uselessly. In the end, even the victor will have been defeated.

If we wish to expand our consciousness, we must first overcome our polarity

We Can Learn From the Elements

It is worthwhile for us to once again take a look at the elements. Water is so soft and yet, at the same time, so hard. We cannot grab hold of it and yet it can dissolve the hardest stone. It wants to dissolve because it wants to merge and become one with all. We can learn so much from these simple elements: to understand that we must liberate ourselves from our polar way of thinking; and to realize that the term "positive" is not to be equated with "good" and "negative" not to be equated with "bad." The terms stand for the polar realm that we adhere to.

Recognize
disease as your
opportunity
to create a
necessary change

Being confronted with these polarities – in the positive or negative sense – it is not for us to judge them as good or bad. The confrontation is taking place in order for us to become aware of our own polarity within the antagonism and to achieve a higher state of consciousness through the process of equalization. In math, plus + and minus – equalize each other harmoniously; they don't fight against each other. The dominating principle is not "either or," but rather "both," and "as well as."

Understanding Disease as Your Friend

Become aware that every disadvantage conceals a much greater advantage. This is how you can understand disease as your best friend. Because this friend candidly informs us when we have done something wrong. This friend simply wants to help you become more aware of yourself and your body. So do not suppress your friend. Let him speak, and learn his language, so that you can exchange information with him. And know that it is never too late for change. It is only too late when we refrain from action because we think it is too late. Bringing this philosophical excursion to an end, let's return to water and salt.

The Creation of Life

When water and salt merge, a new dimension is created–the *sole*.

Atoms have higher frequencies/more energy/more information/more intelligence/more consciousness than molecules, cells, organs or human beings.

All life originated in the primordial ocean from the elements water and salt.

Understand disease as a friend who is telling you what you have to change.

We have learned that water and salt are not only absolute necessities for our body but also for our consciousness. Every single element within the salt has its own vibrational pattern that resonates with the vibrational patterns in our body. Also, we have defined disease as an energy deficit. From this, we can conclude that salt can provide exactly those vibration patterns that we yearn for.

The Healing Effects of Sole

The crystalline structure of salt, as *sole*, has such a lasting effect, that its frequency can be maintained within our body for over 24 hours. *Sole* will give our body the exact vibration that it is missing. The quantity of *sole* you drink is not significant, because biophysics is all about quality, not quantity. Cardinal is the quality of the salt from which you make your *sole*.

For sole *therapy, the quality of the salt used to make it is more important than the quantity of* sole *you drink*

Drink one teaspoon of *sole* in natural spring water every morning on an empty stomach. Again, it is not the quantity that you consume, but the regularity with which you consume it. Bio-chemically, the stomach and intestinal activity (peristaltic) is stimulated within minutes, which in return stimulates your metabolism and digestion. Electrolytes are created which improve the body's conductivity and stimulate the circulation. Salt allows the current to flow.

Sole has a Balancing Effect

Contrary to common table salt, *sole* is not "off limits" for those with high blood pressure. In fact, *sole* lowers the blood pressure within 15 minutes. But this does not mean that *sole* is a blood pressure lowering remedy. Because those with low blood pressure can also drink *sole* and their blood pressure will rise. The *sole's* fundamental attribute is its ability to restore balance. If

*It is not the quantity
but the regularity
with which you drink
the sole*

people with high blood pressure are advised to refrain from using salt, which salt are they referring to? For common table salt, this is true. But not for the salt having holistic properties. Very often, a lack of salt in our body can have negative effects. Again, when we speak of salt, we are talking about real, whole, pure crystal salt. In the U.S., the results of a four-year study showed that people with poor salt concentration in their urine were 4 times more likely to suffer from heart attacks than those with normal salt concentration in their urine. Another study with animals showed slower growth for those whose feed contained reduced amounts of salt.

Sole for Harmonizing Our Acid-Alkaline (pH) Balance

Sole is an exceptional restorative for harmonizing your acid-alkaline balance. *Sole* also flushes out heavy metals in our body such as mercury, lead, arsenic and amalgam, as well as calcification, because the crystal salt breaks apart molecular compounds. Try this simple experiment: Dilute some *sole* in water. Pour this into your electric hot-water kettle and, while the water boils, watch how the limestone on the heating rods dissolves. It may look like magic, but it's a simple chemical and physical reaction. The energetic structure and the ional effect of the crystal salt in the *sole* break apart the molecular compounds and hydrate the elements individually. Allow your body to undergo a similar treatment. Free it from heavy metals, toxins, waste, mucous plaque in your intestines and other waste materials. In order for the body to eliminate these substances, they must first be metabolized.

Crystal salt can dissolve heavy metals in your body and remove them

Initial Aggravation of the Symptoms During the Cleanse

The effects of crystal salt on the body are opposite to the effects of medication. Medications suppress symptoms, while the salt absolutely supports the expression of the symptoms. Plus, it energizes those symptoms that might still be latent in your body and lets you experience them fully. This process oftentimes results in an initial aggravation of the symptoms, as with homeopathy. People with rheumatic illnesses such as gout, arthritis or rheumatoid arthritis, having already developed deposits in their joints, should regularly drink sole to keep the body within the frequency pattern. This will result in the body slowly breaking down the deposits, metabolizing and releasing them. The same therapy applies to kidney and gallbladder stones. The passing of the loosened, dissolved stones can be painful but the body will have managed the process on its own, without surgery.

Drinking sole can loosen and break down deposits in the body.

Cleansing Happens Rhythmically

The body will cleanse itself in rhythms, receiving the necessary energy for its regeneration from the *sole*. This is oftentimes unpleasant for the patient. However, this is the only manner in which the body can loosen and release waste and pollutants that do not belong in the body. Water and salt will do a major clean-up! If, due to wrong dietary habits, too much rotten and fermented substance has accumulated in the intestines, initially the *sole* treatment might cause diarrhea. This is a positive sign that your intestines are being flushed out and cleansed.

How Sole Affects Addictions

Not only alcohol and nicotine are addictive substances, but also the denaturalized foods such as white sugar

For anyone undergoing withdrawal from abusive substances, *sole*-drinking therapy can offer support. A study of heroin addicts conducted in Zürich, Switzerland, showed that the craving for the addictive substance decreased significantly when the withdrawal was supported with *sole* therapy. Most addicts believe they are addicted to a specific substance. The sugar addict thinks his body is yearning for sugar. But in fact, the opposite is true. What we're actually longing for is that which was removed from the natural substance during its manufacturing process! Refined products such as white sugar are isolated compounds. Isolated foods, which have had their holistic properties altered during the denaturalization process, cause the body to react by sending out messages to search for the extracted substances in order to metabolize the food. This is why whole, natural foods, in comparison to processed foods, are of cardinal importance for our health. Isolated and refined food products are essentially addictive. The neutralizing and energetically balancing effect of the *sole* will decrease the yearning for the extracted, missing substances. This can be observed in children who are addicted to sugar. You will see how your child's sugar craving will decrease when you add *sole* to his/her drinking water on a daily basis.

Sole – A Balm for our Skin

Sole is an excellent remedy for skin disease and is also used in allopathic medicine. Anyone ever having had problems with their skin is familiar with the healing properties of the ocean, specifically with neurodermatitis and psoriasis. The skin is an excretive organ that mirrors the condition of our intestines. *Sole* will give your body the ability to cleanse itself from the inside as well as from the outside. Initial aggravation of the skin, rashes and diarrhea can occur as the *sole* creates a foundation for the skin to regain its general condition of health. But after some time, your skin will reflect the healthy condition of your inner body and begin to radiate this vital, living energy.

Sometimes, the symptoms may aggravate while the body reestablishes its balance

The Healing Effects of Sole

Sole-drinking therapy restores the body's natural frequency pattern and can hold this vibration for over 24 hours.

Sole balances the acid-alkaline imbalance as well as normalizing the blood pressure.

Sole dissolves and releases crystallized deposits, the cause of rheumatic diseases and kidney and gallbladder stones.

Sole weakens addictions.

Sole cleans the intestines and heals skin diseases.

The

Forms

The Various Applications of Salt

In the last chapters we have learned a lot about the value and the effects of water and salt. In the following chapter we will elaborate on the numerous water and salt applications. We will explain how to prepare *sole*, guide you through an inhalation therapy and point out aspects to consider when taking a *sole* bath or flushing your system with sole. Furthermore, we will reveal to you many naturopathic remedies consisting only of water and salt. You will also learn about floatation tanks, about the effects of crystal salt ionizers and crystal salt lamps on our whole being and their appropriate uses, as well as several skin and body care applications for *sole*.

> Water and salt affect our mind and spirit as well as our body

Initiate Change Consciously

When you decide to apply some of the *sole* remedies at home, we ask that you not simply follow the procedures, but also that you become consciously aware of the magnificent reformation that you are initiating in your life with the help of the primal elements, water and salt. Even though you will primarily experience the effects on a physical level, they will also have implications on an energetic, subtle level for both your mind and spirit. Have patience. Give yourself the time and tranquility for attaining health and remaining healthy from within. Be aware of the possibility of an initial aggravation of your condition, and let your family and friends know what you are doing, so they can support you.

Preparing the Crystal Sole

Place several crystal salt stones in a small glass jar with a lid, preferably glass but not metal. Plastic is ok. You can use a thoroughly cleaned jam or "ball" jar for example. Cover the salt crystals with pure, living spring water, like FIJI Water or your quartz crystal charged spring water. After about two hours, check to see if the crystals have dissolved. If they have completely dissolved, add another crystal salt stone. Keep doing this until the water can no longer dissolve any more salt, and the crystal salt stones remains at the bottom of the jar. The water has reached its 26% salt saturation level. You now have *sole*.

At this point, the salt crystals will no longer dissolve until you add more water. Once the solution arrives at 26% (26 parts of salt to 100 parts of water), it is saturated and becomes *sole*. Therefore, you must look to see that there are always salt crystals remaining at the bottom of the jar, as an indicator that this solution is saturated!

You can always add water to the jar to replenish your supply of *sole*. Just remember, once the crystals have fully dissolved, you must add more crystals so that there are always undissolved salt crystals left in the *sole*. In this way you always know that the *sole* is fully saturated. This jar of *sole* doesn't need to be stored in any special manner, wherever it is convenient for you. The *sole* is a sterile solution and naturally prevents all kinds of germs, viruses, bacteria or fungi from forming in the jar.

Sole is fundamental for many of the following applications.

The salt crystals are dissolved in water until they reach a 26% solution – sole

Sole Drinking

Important is not the quantity in which the *sole* is taken, but rather the regularity, and of course the quality of the *sole*; the potential of energy/information held within its crystalline lattice. Using a teaspoon as a unit of measure is more of an index. From a biochemical perspective, 1 teaspoon of crystal salt *sole* is the amount needed by the body. Biophysically, a few drops of sole would be sufficient to hold the frequency for at least 24 hours. The regularity of the application is much more important than the quantity, because our body regenerates itself rhythmically. Therefore, using the term drinking therapy is actually inappropriate because it implies the notion of a limit. However, we will continue to use the word, keeping in mind that it bears no limits. We highly recommend adopting this therapy of one teaspoon of *sole* per day

It is not the quantity but the quality of the *sole* you drink

Put one teaspoon of sole in a glass of good quality spring water

as a lifetime habit. Additionally, you should fully renounce other salts and replace them with crystal salt. Remember that most canned and processed foods contain refined, processed salt as a preservative. If you do not want to give up using these products, it would be advisable to add a little bit of crystal salt to them to reduce the aggressive effects of the sodium chloride.

Instructions for the Sole Drinking Therapy

Add one teaspoon of 26% percent *sole* to a glass of good quality spring water.

Drink this every morning on an empty stomach. You can also extend this application by adding one teaspoon of *sole* to a quart of water and drink it throughout the day.

If the cleansing effect is too intense, you can reduce the amount of *sole* to a couple of drops, rather than a teaspoon per day. This depends on your individual constitution and judgement.

the amount of *sole* to a couple of drops, rather than a teaspoon per day. This depends on your individual constitution and judgment.

For children and babies, a few drops of sole are sufficient.

The less salty the *sole* solution, the more likely your child is to drink it. Adding a couple drops of *sole* to your child's meal is adequate.

The frequency pattern of the salt in the *sole* will be retained in your body for up to 24 hours.

Sole Inhalation

For inhalation therapy, the ratio between water and salt should be at least 1%, which equals 0.35 ounces of salt per quart of water. However, experience has shown that especially with diseases affecting the deeper respiratory pathways, higher concentrations of up to 8% achieve better result. The concentration should be slowly increased, starting with a 1% *sole* solution.

Instructions for the Sole Inhalation

Fill a wide pot or pan with one to two quarts of water and heat until it begins to steam.

Add at least 0.7 ounces of coarse or crushed crystal salt. After the salt dissolves, cover your head with a large towel and, holding your face over the pot far enough so as not to burn yourself, inhale deeply.

Inhale the *sole* steam for 10 to 15 minutes.

Following the inhalation, the respiratory organs need approximately 30 minutes to accumulate and bind the pollutants in mucous so it can be coughed up.

This procedure can be repeated several times a day according to your needs, until the symptoms recede.

Flushing the Sinus with Sole

For sinus flushing, use a neti-pot which is designed specifically for this function. For this application of sinus flushing, prepare a 1% *sole* solution by dissolving 0.35 ounces of crystal salt in

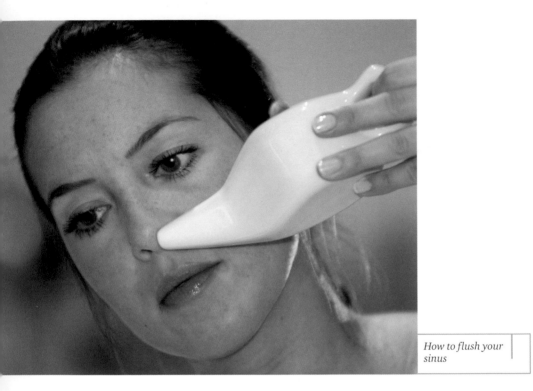

3.4 ounces of lukewarm water. This concentration is equal to the salt concentration in our body fluids and hence does not irritate the nose as does seawater. This application can be repeated as often as necessary but usually twice a day is sufficient to keep your sinus clear.

Instructions for a Sinus Flush

Lean your head over the bathroom sink and apply the beak of the neti-pot into your nostril. Keep your mouth closed.

Slightly lean your head forward and bend it to one side. The *sole* will flow through your nostril and come out of the other nostril. Repeat this procedure with the other nostril.

This 1% *sole* solution is also excellent for gargling when infections of the mucous membranes in the nose, mouth and throat areas occur.

For an eye bath, you can find eye-wash cups in pharmacies and health food stores. For this application you also prepare a 1% lukewarm *sole* solution, similar to the one used for sinus flushing.

Instructions for an Eye Bath

Please remove all make-up thoroughly before washing the eyes.

Pour a 1% *sole* solution into the eye-wash cup and hold the cup close to your eye so that no liquid can escape. (Pics. A and B) Gently tip your head back, washing the solution over the eye while simultaneously opening and closing your eye repeatedly, so that the *sole* solution can saturate your eye. (Pic. C)

While keeping your eye open, roll it around for several minutes.

A

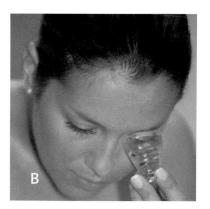
B

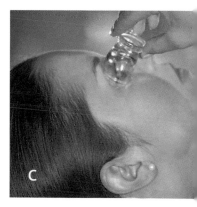
C

The Sole Bath

In contrast to a normal bath, in which moisture is extracted from the skin, a sole bath allows salt to be stored in the upper callous layer of the skin and binds water. This maintains the natural, protective film of the skin, protecting it from drying out. This is the reason why *sole* baths are good for dry skin as well. The cleansing effects of a 30-minute sole bath equal those of three days of fasting. The toxins are released into the bath water through osmosis, while the minerals from the *sole* are absorbed through the skin. This reduces the acidity in our body and balances the pH factor of our skin. Studies have shown that you can achieve the best results taking a *sole* bath during the change of the moon cycle. The minerals and energies stored in the sole can optimally be absorbed during a full moon. The body's healing potential is at its peak, bioenergetically weak points are harmonized, and the body's own energy flow is activated. During a new moon, the cleansing effects are optimized because the body's capacity for detoxifying is at an optimum. The bath will have a detoxifying effect similar to a three-day fast.

A 30-minute sole bath has the cleansing effect of a three-day fast

Activate Your Self-Healing Powers

This *sole* bath is a sheer ocean of energy for us. Bioenergetic deficits are rebalanced and weak links become strengthened, reactivating our body's electric current. The organs' functions begin to resonate with the natural frequency patterns of the *sole*. This activates the natural regulatory mechanism of the body and its self-healing powers. The concentration of the *sole* bath can slowly be increased from 1% to 8%. The higher the concentration, the stronger the cleansing effect, and the more severe will be the body's reaction.

How to Prepare a Sole Bath

You can find numerous bath salts on the shelves of many stores. Most of these have been chemically treated and therefore lost their natural qualities. Ideally, for a salt-bath treatment you should try to obtain natural, untreated crystal salt. This salt can be found in natural, cotton bags that contain 1 kilogram (just over 2 pounds) of crystal salt. Pour the entire contents of the bag into your bathtub and add enough water to just cover it. After about ten minutes the salt will be dissolved. Now you can fill your bathtub. Do not add any other bath products to a *sole* bath.

The bath water should have a temperature of approximately 98.6°F, our normal body temperature. Check the temperature with a thermometer. This is important, as the body must not additionally sacrifice its own energy to balance out the temperature. The bath water will remain at 98.6°F almost continuously. This is because the biophysical structure of the *sole* solution is so strong; it causes the molecules to move in a constant rhythm. In temperature and makeup, this sole bath is comparable to the amniotic fluid in which the embryo floats in the prenatal state. Now the boundaries are fading which separate your body from the *sole* solution in which you are floating. *Sole* baths have a positive effect on numerous ailments. They are, however, demanding on the circulatory system. Be aware of this if you suffer from weak or poor heart circulation and consult your doctor beforehand. If a full bath would be too strenuous for you, you can take a footbath.

A sole bath will replenish your lost energy

Instructions for a Sole Bath

The *sole* bath should have a minimum salt concentration of 1%. For an average bathtub, with 28-gallons capacity, you would need 2.35 pounds (1 kilo) of crystal salt. If your tub had a larger capacity, you would accordingly need to use more salt. The formula for a **1%** solution is **1.28** ounces of salt per gallon of water.

Do not use any bath additives, soaps or oils.

You should soak between **15-30** minutes.

Do not shower off, simply dry off with a towel.

After the *sole* bath you should rest at least **30** minutes.

Floatation

The floatation-tank *sole* bath is a special kind of bath. Floating in a crystal salt ocean, enclosed within the tank, is an extraordinary experience. Liberated from time, you travel deep into your innermost self. The crystal salt floatation tank is a further development of the "Samadhi Tank" and the "Float Spa" applications. Dr John Lilly studied the human body in a state of zero gravity back in the 1950's. His research initially served to provide NASA with a method for simulating zero gravity in their astronaut-training program. All floatation tanks are based on the same principle of floating in a sensory deprivation environment of highly concentrated saltwater.

The floatation tank simulates a state of zero gravity and, creates a sense of existence outside of time and space

Floating in a Quasi-Prenatal State

Whilst floating, you are completely isolated from the outside world, because the tank deprives you of all external stimuli. Additionally, the *sole* in which you are floating, and the tank itself, maintain the same temperature as your body, so it doesn't have to provide its own energy to balance the temperature. Through decades of research, John Lilly demonstrated that, even when our senses are deprived, our brain is still active because our subconscious is always active. Initially, magnesium sulfate was used for the salt solution in the tank. However, biophysical research with natural salt paved the way for the use of crystal salt, rather than a processed substance, to provide the salty environment within the tank. This change allows for a true quasi-prenatal state in the tank, because the body now floats in a natural energetic frequency spectrum that resembles its original condition inside the womb. This condition allows us to be consciously aware of our own self.

How Floatation Affects the System

The effects that the floatation tank has on our consciousness can be quite profound. We float in a *sole* solution like that from

The floatation tank puts us in a quasi-prenatal state

which we originally came, in our mother's womb. Protected from all outside influence, we are suspended in our own liquid cocoon. Quiet, warm and safe, we experience a return to our prenatal state. This can be quite profound for many. Some people have out-of-body experiences during a 60-minute float session – this also has a significant impact on our health.

Dr Lilly found that you can create a sense of well-being: "Somewhere deep within the brain, was a mechanism capable of generating internal experiences completely independent of the outside world, and this settled the issue of what happens in profound physical isolation. The isolated mind becomes highly active and creative."

Releasing Blockages through Deep Relaxation

The remarkable effects of floatation go even further. Floatation results in an increase in physical performance. Top athletes have long known about and taken advantage of this benefit. The deep relaxation provided by the floatation remedies sore muscles by reducing the production of lactic acid and increasing the production of beta-endorphins. Furthermore, our coordinative abilities improve and our consciousness expands, which further releases energetic and emotional blockages in

The Effects of Floatation

Extensive scientific studies have shown that floatation in a sensory deprivation tank is an extraordinary good way of relieving stress. Floatation normalizes the blood pressure, regardless of whether it is too high or too low.

Rheumatic ailments are reduced. The immune system is strengthened. Oftentimes, floating results in weight reduction.

Floating inside an oceanic solution that resembles our physical body, and entirely deprived of exterior stimuli, we are able to regenerate completely.

Floatation stimulates the production of endorphins, the "so-called" happiness hormones and strengthens our overall sense of well-being.

The state of deep relaxation regulates our breathing and our blood circulation, allowing for extraordinary healing effects through the absence of gravity. Body, mind and spirit will experience their individuality in ways beyond comparison, and our batteries are completely recharged.

Floatation is an extraordinary therapy for effectively reducing stress and providing relief for many other ailments our body. Floatation balances our brain hemispheres, which heightens and increases our creativity. Some compare the one-hour floating session to a vacation because we return from the experience totally relaxed, like having visited the most wonderful place on earth. We should treat ourselves at least once in our life to a floatation experience in crystal salt sole inside a sensory deprivation tank. You can find more information about floatation tanks in the Resources section at the back of this book.

Topical Application of Sole

Top athletes, executives, and artists alike, appreciate the extraordinary effects of the floatation tank

Topical applications of *sole* are mainly used for skin diseases, injuries, insect bites, pain and injuries of the soft tissues, and joints, as well as for de-acidification. The strength of the concentration depends on the ailment and whether or not it involves treating an open wound. Generally speaking, the more extreme the injury, the more concentrated you make the *sole* preparation. Open wounds should only be treated with a 1% *sole* solution, to avoid burning. Use one part salt in 100 parts of water, i.e. 0.035 ounces (weight) of crystal salt in 3.5 ounces (volume) of water. It is advisable to use good spring water on open wounds and to avoid tap water. The *sole* solution can be increased in concentration up to 8%. Bruises, sprains or swellings can be saturated with a *sole* concentration of up to 26%. This also applies to insect bites and herpes blisters.

Sole can also be used as a treatment for poisons oak, ivy and sumac. The natural antibacterial qualities of the *sole* can help to keep bacterial infections from arising. The *sole* will have a soothing effect on the skin. You will experience much relief from the itching, and you will feel less need to scratch yourself. If you already have open sores from scratching,

Topical applications of sole regulate the storage of fatty tissue and balance the pH of the skin

For open wounds always use only a 1% *sole* solution

only apply a 1% *sole* solution. Otherwise, you can apply the *sole* in concentrations up to 26%. The *sole* can be applied as often as needed. You can also apply a *sole* topical to the severely infected areas.

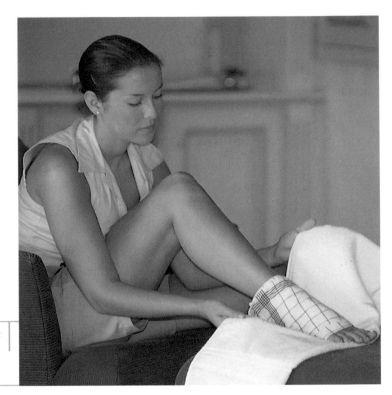

Sole Wraps

For open wounds use only a 1% *sole* solution. For injuries of the soft tissues or ailments of the joints you can use a *sole* concentration between 3% and 10%. Cold thigh wraps soaked in *sole* are most effective for lowering fever. Use a clean linen or cotton towel and soak it in a *sole* solution of recommended concentration; wring it well and wrap it around your thighs.

The Salt Shirt

The Salt Shirt is a specific variant of the "Spanish Coat" used by Sebastian Kneipp. It has exceptional detoxifying effects and

Instructions for Salt Shirt Application

Soak a clean cotton, long sleeved shirt in a 3% sole solution or 3 Tbsp. of crystal salt diluted in 1 quart of water. Wring it well and put it on.

Wrap yourself in a large, dry bath towel or bathrobe and lie in bed. Cover yourself with blankets. Within half an hour you will begin to sweat.

After 60-90 minutes, take off the shirt and shower.

activates the metabolism. The Salt Shirt has also proven to be an effective treatment for flu and high fever as an alternative to the *sole* bath. Drinking a cup of linden tea while on this treatment has supportive effects.

Salt Socks

The salt socks therapy works exactly like the salt shirt therapy and has proven to be effective for treating gout and chronically cold feet.

Instructions for Salt Socks Application

Soak a clean pair of cotton socks in a 3-5% sole solution or 2-4 Tbsp. of crystal salt in 1 quart of water. Wring them well, put them on and wrap your feet in a dry towel. For full effect of this application, keep them wrapped on for one hour.

Salt Satchet Applications

The salt satchet provides warmth where needed, e.g., for ear infections, tense and sore muscles, and back and joint pains. Under no circumstances should you use this application for acute, infectious rheumatic pains or for an acute gout attack!

Instructions for Salt-Sachet Application

Heat the dry salt sachet in the oven (Do not microwave!) at around and 120-140° F and apply the sachet to the troubled area for about 20 minutes.

Body Peeling

The body peeling, made from a mixture of salt and oil, is ideal for detoxifying. The effects are similar to several days of fasting. You can buy these salt-oil mixtures ready-made (e.g., Water&Salt Peeling), or prepare them yourself.

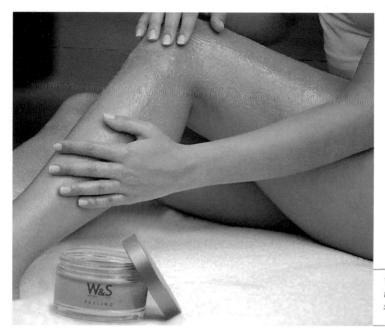

With a salt peeling, the skin detoxifies and stores moisture

Instructions for Body Peeling

Mix 2 to 3 Tbsp. of coarse crushed crystal salt with the same amount of natural oil, e.g. Macadamia Nut Oil, Jojoba Oil, Cocoa Oil or Sesame Oil.

Lie down on a large towel or linen sheet and let someone apply the mixture to your body. Make sure the mixture is stirred with a spoon each time it is applied.

Wrap yourself in the towel or the sheet cover yourself with a blanket. Let your body absorb the peeling for at least half an hour. You will start to feel pleasant warmth as your cells start working.

Rinse off with lukewarm water and gently dab yourself dry.

The sole mud mask
supports the skin's
natural regulation

Peloid (Sole Mud)

Crystal *sole* "peloid" is the natural, mineral-rich, soft, wet earth that accumulates on the floor of the salt mine and re-crystallizes. These crystalline components are mined, finely ground and mixed with natural crystal *sole*. The crystal *sole* peloid can re-hydrate dehydrated cells. It is effective in treating skin irritations, tissue injuries as well as cellulite. The crystal *sole* mud effectively supports the natural regeneration of the skin. It neutralizes skin impurities, prevents the forming of wrinkles and tightens the upper layer of your skin.

Peloid is a natural product, made exclusively out of crystal salt that was extracted from the salt mines of Berchtesgaden, Germany. It is commercially available as Water&Salt Peloid. For ordering information, please refer to the Product Suppliers section at the end of this book.

Instructions for Facial mask

Exclude the eyes and lips when applying a facial mask. Let the mask be absorbed for 15-20 minutes. Rinse with water and dab it dry, do not rub.

In addition, the *sole* peloid is useful for all kinds of infectious reactions of the body, especially in cases when a cold-press would be helpful.

Instructions for Sole Mud Wrap

Apply the crystal *sole* peloid on the problem area.

If you wish to make a cold-press, wrap a cold, wet towel around the peloid and let it be absorbed for several hours. Rinse off with cold water.

The crystal ionizer creates a sole fog

Crystal Salt Ionizer

This is a novel ultrasound device, which not only stimulates the water, but also activates the *sole* to the extent that the molecular compounds separate from the water. The disconnected water molecules then bind the salt in its ionized form, due to its specific frequency. Without heating the water, this creates a *sole* fog, producing an ocean-front climate. It cleanses the air because it binds the positively charged dust particles. Furthermore, it creates a neutral frequency in the room within two hours. Besides the ionizing effect, your body is surrounded by a vibration pattern identical to its own. The relaxation and balance that your system realizes is similar to that found at the beach or in a salt chamber.

The crystal salt ionizer creates a climate similar to that found at the seashore

How to use the Ionizer

In preparing the *sole* for the ionizer, use spring water with very low mineral content or distilled water. Mix two pints of water with one heaping teaspoon of crystal salt.

Make sure there is always adequate liquid in the bowl so as not to damage the device.

The fog it creates is ideal for inhalation. It's sufficient to use the ionizer for only two or three hours at a time, for instance, a couple of hours before going to bed.

A crystal salt ionizer is similar to a water fog machine. However, the fog machine is pure decoration, whereas the crystal salt ionizer is therapeutic and specifically intended for ionizing the *sole*, creating a completely different, distinct frequency than the fog machine.

Crystal Salt Lamps

A crystal salt lamp produces effects similar to those of the *sole* ionizer, although on a smaller scale. However, crystal salt lamps have big advantages, in many aspects, and not only for cleaning the environment of a room. Sitting in front of televisions or computer monitors, we are bombarded with an electro-magnetic frequency of around 100 to 160 Hz (Hertz). Our brainwaves however, vibrate at around 8 Hz, a rate that equals the Schuhmann-Resonance-Frequency. This means that while watching TV or working at the computer, our body is exposed to frequencies that vibrate twenty times faster than our brainwaves. The result is a lack of concentration, nervousness and insomnia. Furthermore, the body produces additional free radicals that, amongst other things, can cause cancer.

Harmonizing Ionizing Effect

Crystal salt lamps bind excessive positive ions with their negative ions. When they warm up, they attract humidity, and the surface of the salt crystal becomes moist. This causes a field of ions to build up. Crystal salt lamps can also neutralize the electro-smog in a room. Additionally, the various colors of the lamp have positive therapeutic effects. Their wavelengths fall within the upper nanometer zone (600 to 700 nanometers), which are visible to our eyes and effect a reorganization of the epidermal layer of the skin. The frequencies in this upper nanometer zone are also used in allopathic medicine for treating skin cancer. Furthermore, tests on hyperactive children with concentration and sleeping disorders (ADHD symptoms) have shown that using crystal salt lamps drastically reduces their

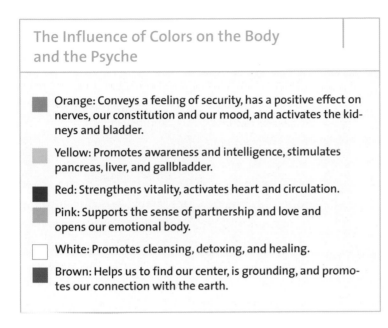

The Influence of Colors on the Body and the Psyche

- Orange: Conveys a feeling of security, has a positive effect on nerves, our constitution and our mood, and activates the kidneys and bladder.

- Yellow: Promotes awareness and intelligence, stimulates pancreas, liver, and gallbladder.

- Red: Strengthens vitality, activates heart and circulation.

- Pink: Supports the sense of partnership and love and opens our emotional body.

- White: Promotes cleansing, detoxing, and healing.

- Brown: Helps us to find our center, is grounding, and promotes our connection with the earth.

symptoms after only one week. When the lamps were removed, the symptoms returned.

Beware of Copycats

The salt used for making crystal salt lamps can easily be mistaken for having properties similar to the crystal salt we have been talking about throughout this book. Many lamps use salt that came from salt mines in either Poland or Pakistan, where crystal salt doesn't necessarily possess the biophysical properties required for physiological use. When we talk about crystal salt in this book, we are referring to that particular crystal salt which has been subject to extensive scientific research, and originates in the Himalayan Mountains. The crystal salt from Polish and Pakistani mines are suitable for the production of crystal salt lamps, but not for the applications mentioned in this book, or for internal use.

Crystal salt lamps emit therapeutic, electromagnetic wavelengths of colors known to positively impact our body and mind

The

Applications

Practical Examples of Salt Applications

We learned about natural crystal salt as a food source, as having neutralizing and balancing effects on our body due to its unique characteristics, and for imparting new energy to our body. There is hardly a more efficient and natural remedy than crystal salt, in combination with good, mature spring water, to stimulate our body's innate regulatory abilities and restore our energy balance. As a result of these inherent properties, crystal salt has a positive, beneficial effect on all diseases. In principle, it is incorrect to speak of diseases when, in reality, there is only one disease: energy deficit. This energy deficit manifests itself in numerous ways. If our energy reserves aren't replenished, our body cannot regenerate itself, resulting in deposits and in alterations of the tissue, which occur in several organs.

There is only
one disease:
energy deficit

Don't Suppress the Symptom – Remove the Cause

Modern allopathic medicine is oriented to relieving symptoms rather than removing the cause of disease. Allopathic medications impair the ability of our body to regenerate itself. And, besides their damaging side-effects, they suppress the body's innate abilty of self-healing. Beware, however, that your body will have become accustomed to certain medications if you have been taking them for a while. Seek the advice of a naturopathic doctor, chiropractor or therapist who you

The skin: mirror of our body and soul

trust and who is open-minded to holistic healing methods. The following chapter discusses several valuable applications of crystal salt. In the appendix you will find useful information and resources.

The Skin

Our skin protects us from outer influences and is our body's largest excretive organ. Our skin mirrors our body and our soul. Mistakenly, it is thought that our skin has an acid protection coat, a notion that is promoted by the cosmetic industry. However, their products actually acidify our body even more, because our skin does not have an acid protection coat. The pH factors used to reason the existence of this protective coat are average values from studies with subjects who were already overlay acid. The inner acidity is mirrored in the skin. Our skin, as our entire body, needs neutral pH factors. Crystal salt can regulate the pH of the skin optimally and in the long term, through its balancing, neutralizing effects. A healthy body has natural healthy skin. If you use any additional substances, make sure they are of high quality and designed to support the skin's own self-healing capabilities, e.g. products from the Water&Salt Body Care series. We are more prone to skin problems, such as acne or allergies, if we eat a lot of animal protein in the form of eggs, fish, meat and dairy. It is important to drink the *sole* in addition to the topical salt applications. Until inner balance is reached, the topical applications have a supportive effect.

Crystal salt balances the pH of our skin

Acne, Unhealthy Skin, Eczema

These skin diseases are mentioned together because they require identical treatment. We have mentioned that the skin is a mirror of our body and, foremost, of our intestine. Skin

The aging of the skin is mainly due to a loss of cell fluid

Flawed skin, especially around the mouth, is always an indication of disturbed intestinal flora

irritations and eczema appearing around the neckline and in the face, especially around the mouth area, always indicate a disrupted intestinal flora. The body cannot eliminate its toxins and, hence, excretes them through the skin. A change of diet, together with a colon cleanse, is necessary to eliminate the cause. At the same time, it is also important to drink plenty of living spring water, low in minerals, in order to flush out the waste material. An additional salt therapy will "work wonders."

This application works for dry and oily skin alike because of the balancing properties of the salt. After this treatment your skin will have been replenished with natural moisture and has attained attained a balanced pH. In order to maintain this condition, it is recommended to apply a peloid mask (*sole* mud) once or twice a month.

Salt Applications for Infectious Skin Diseases

Drink one teaspoon of *sole* in a glass of living spring water every morning on an empty stomach.

Drink two to three quarts of low mineral and non-carbonated water per day.

Once daily, apply concentrated *sole* to the troubled areas allowing it to absorb into the skin. If you must use creams, only choose high-quality products, such as Water&Salt Skin Care.

Apply a peloid mask (*sole* mud) twice a week and let it soak in for 15-20 minutes before removing the mask with a wet washcloth.

Initial worsening of the skin's condition is possible. However, once this phase passes, the skin improves dramatically.

Neurodermatitis

Neurodermatitis belongs to the family of allergic disorders and can appear as early as infancy. Symptoms can first be noticed as scabs on the top of a baby's head. Most of the time this disorder surfaces when the mother stops breast-feeding or is not able to breast feed and the baby is fed with cow milk. The primary cause of neurodermatitis in babies is an inherited allergy to cow's milk. In some severe cases, neurodermatitis can occur when the mother includes dairy products in her diet while she is breast-feeding the baby. In such cases the mother should immediately give up all dairy products. Later on, these children may have eczema in specific areas, for example on the inside of the bend of their knees and elbows or on their entire bodies. With adults, it is often found on the hands, and in severe cases the eczema covers the entire body. The skin is brittle, dry and itchy. In addition to the salt therapy, naturopathic treatment might be necessary. We would like to give just one more recommendation for treating neurodermatitis in general: try to avoid dairy products, animal proteins and wheat products as well as sugar and all processed foods. These changes in your diet will improve the condition tremendously. Initially, your skin condition may take a turn for the worse, and diarrhea is a common side effect. But don't worry. This

Salt Applications for Neurodermatitis

Drink one teaspoon of *sole* in a glass of living spring water every morning on an empty stomach. A few drops of *sole* are sufficient for babies.

Drink two to three quarts of low mineral and non-carbonated water per day.

A crystal salt bath will alleviate the itch. The concentration of salt depends on the condition of your skin. If you have any open sores, please only use a 1% concentration = one part salt to 100 parts of bath water or 1 kilo of salt in 28 gallons of water. A children's tub holds about 5-8 gallons of water in which you would put 7-10 ounces (weight) of salt.

You can increase the concentration up to 5%. Besides alleviating the itch, a *sole* bath also adds moisture to the skin and relaxes the central nervous system.

For a severe condition, take a *sole* bath twice a week. After the skin has normalized, taking a *sole* bath once to twice a month is sufficient.

will soon pass and is a positive sign that the intestine is getting rid of putrefied and fermented substances.

Psoriasis

Psoriasis is a genetically inherited disease and usually doesn't manifest until adulthood. The accelerated growth of the topical layer of skin forms red spots, which are usually covered with a thick layer of white flakes. Normally, it takes twenty-eight

The salt water of the oceans helps to relieve the symptoms of psoriasis

With psoriasis, an alkaline diet is the foundation for all treatments (see food chart on page 43)

days for our epidermal layer to be fully replaced, the time it takes for the deep skin cells to move through to the top layer. With people suffering from psoriasis, this process happens in only four days, and it can cause severe itching, too. The fact that one may be genetically predisposed to this disease doesn't rule out the possibility for completely healing the disorder. An alkaline-forming, vegan diet, in combination with salt therapy, can work wonders. Allopathic medicine is familiar with the healing effects of salt therapy for psoriasis. In many cases doctors prescribe bathing in highly concentrated bodies of salt water, like the Dead Sea, with the highest salt concentration on Earth. However, these treatments only provide temporary relief, and the symptoms reoccur when the patient returns home. Now, we can bring the ocean into our homes!

Salt Applications for Psoriasis

Drink one teaspoon of *sole* in a glass of living spring water every morning on an empty stomach.

Drink two to three quarts of low mineral and non-carbonated water daily.

Since the skin of a person suffering from psoriasis is usually not open, but infectious and thickened, a higher concentrated *sole* bath is recommended. Begin with a 3% solution or 3 kilos of salt

➤

➤

in 26 gallons of bath water. The concentration can be increased up to 8% (7.5 kilos of salt). The *sole* bath adds moisture to the skin and alleviates the infection.

A highly concentrated *sole* bath is exhausting for the circulation, especially at higher temperatures. Therefore, make sure the temperature of the water is at, or preferably below, 98.6º F.

Make sure that another person is around, to help you in case of circulation problems.

Do not rinse after bathing; gently dab your skin dry.

Take a sole bath twice per week for about 10 to 20 minutes.

Sunbathing is a complementary therapy. You may also use a UV-lamp as an alternative. The skin should be moist when you expose it to the sun, Ideally directly following the bath. Please note, however, that salt water makes the skin more sensitive to UV rays. For each side of the body, do not exceed 10 minutes of sunbathing or exposure to UV rays.

Undiluted, saturated *sole* can be directly applied to the red spots. Additionally, you can apply a concentrated sole wrap on those areas.

The application of a Water&Salt Peloid mask (*sole* mud) is helpful, too. Apply the *sole*-mud thinly on the troubled skin spots and let it dry. Wash it off after 15-20 minutes. You can repeat this procedure on a daily basis until the spots have disappeared.

Treat yourself to floatation tank therapy as well. The salt concentration in these tanks is similar to that of the Dead Sea.

Apply the peloid mask thinly on the affected areas

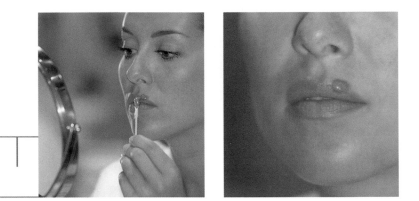

Water&Salt Peloid (sole mask) also relieves Herpes blisters

Herpes Infections

Herpes blisters are unpleasant, painful and, worst of all, recurrent. The herpes virus perpetually resides in our nerve pathways. When our immune system is weak, it propagates explosively and forms the typical blisters. Once they appear, pharmaceutical ointments are of little help. Try applying a Water&Salt Peloid mask. Inwardly, the sole strenghtens your immune system, and outwardly the salt heals the skin quickly.

Salt Applications for Herpes

Drink one teaspoon of *sole* in a glass of living spring water every morning on an empty stomach.

Dab some concentrated *sole* directly on the blister as frequently as once every hour.

Apply Water&Salt Peloid mask onto the blisters before going to bed and leave it on over night. Rinse it off in the morning.

The salt dries out the blisters, kills the viruses and regenerates the skin.

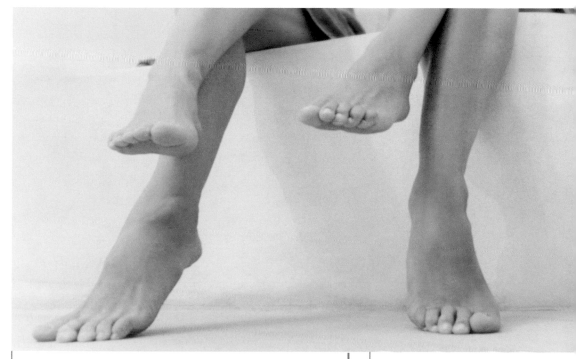

Because athlete's foot results from an acidic condition, it should not be treated only externally

Athlete's Foot

Athlete's foot can be quickly and effectively cured with crystal salt. If toenails are also infested, the treatment can take up to three months, as the nails grow slowly. Anyone having recurring athlete's foot should understand that it is not an infection limited to the feet. The symptom occurs in combination with the growth of a fungus in the intestine or from an acidic metabolism, ideal conditions that promote the growth of foot fungus. The *sole* has a disinfecting effect which keeps the fungus from spreading. Furthermore, the salt regenerates the skin, making it better able to fight against the fungus and other bacteria and viruses.

Salt Application for Athletes Foot

Drink one teaspoon of *sole* in a glass of living spring water every morning on an empty stomach.

Turn to an alkaline-forming, wholesome diet.

Bathe your feet in a concentrated *sole* solution, starting at 10%. Lightly towel your feet dry without rubbing.

If the skin is unopened, apply pure *sole* on the fungus and let it absorb into the skin.

Warts

Warts are not painful, but they are annoying, unpleasant to look at, and very obstinate. Surprisingly, salt will effectively eliminate warts. Warts are caused by viruses and are always an indication of structural disorder, an imbalance in our blood. It is only in such an environment that viruses, fungi or bacteria can proliferate. Therefore, when treating warts it is important to not only treat them externally, but also internally with the *sole* drinking therapy.

Insect Bites

Concentrated *sole* is an excellent remedy for the itching and swelling caused by insect bites, and especially for swelling associated with infection. It can provide especially quick relief from summertime mosquito and horsefly bites. And, because of its soothing and hydrating properties, a 5% solution can also ease the itching and burning of rashes that arise from poisons ivy, oak and sumac.

Salt Applications for Warts

Drink one teaspoon of *sole* in a glass of living spring water every morning on an empty stomach.

Dab the wart with pure *sole* or make a pure sole wrap.

Apply Water&Salt Peloid mask on the warts and wrap a moist towel or linen around it.

If the warts appear on feet or hands, it is recommended to soak them in a highly concentrated *sole* solution of at least 10%. Do not rinse the salt solution after soaking and lightly towel dry without rubbing.

Some warts can disappear within a few days.

Salt Applications for Insect Bites

Lightly rub the insect bites with pure *sole* several times a day or wrap them in a *sole* saturated cloth. This alleviates the itch and removes the swelling.

Water&Salt Peloid mask is another effective remedy. Apply some peloid to the bite and let it dry. Rinse it off after two hours and repeat as often as needed.

Allergies

Allergy-related disorders have rapidly increased in the last decades

Allergy-related disorders have rapidly increased over the last decades and the tendency is, unfortunately, rising. In America alone, every third person suffers from some form of allergy. The causes are believed to be related to immune disorders, genetic heritage, pollution, poor nutrition, increased absorption of chemicals and medication, electro-smog and ozone distress, damage from vaccination and increasing stress. It is also allopathically acknowledged that a prolonged stay within a salt chamber has positive effects on those suffering from asthma and hay fever. The cause is not just the air quality in the a salt chamber, which is very pure, but primarily the frequency pattern of the salt, which replenishes our energy reserves. Since we cannot build our homes in salt mines, we must look for alternative methods for coming into contact with this specific frequency pattern.

Asthma

Asthma is a respiratory disease which causes attacks of suffocation. With bronchial asthma the bronchi have a tendency to

Numerous environmental factors burden our immune system

spasmodically tighten. This can be an occasional attack or, in severe cases, permanent. The problem most often occurs when exhaling. Gasping, dry whistling and rattling sounds accompany the breathing. At the onset of this disease, allergic mechanisms play a central role. As the asthma persists, the more severe is the bronchial system's reaction.

In time, the asthma attack can even occur without any allergenic influence. In some cases, prior viral or bacterial infections

Salt crystals from the healing salt mine in Wieliczka, Poland

Peter Ferreira with two young asthma patients, 226 meters beneath the earth in one of the healing salt chambers of Wieliczka, Poland

of the bronchi laid the ground for the asthma. Chronic lack of water and severe psychological problems can also cause asthma. If you are currently taking medication, please do not discontinue without consulting your physician. This could result in a severe asthma attack. Only after the salt has proven its effects through holistic therapy treatment, the medication can slowly be reduced under supervision of a physician.

Hay Fever and Allergic Eye Infections

Worldwide, the two most common causes of allergy are grass and pollen. Over ten percent of the population of industrialized

Salt Applications for Allergic Asthma

Drink one teaspoon of *sole* in a glass of living spring water every morning on an empty stomach.

Drink two to three quarts of low mineral and non-carbonated water per day.

Inhalation with a salt solution is a time-tested household remedy for asthma. Start out with a 1% *sole* solution. This can be increased up to 3%. Follow this procedure once to twice a day for 15 minutes.

Sole is also suitable for use in inhalation devices. The temperature of the solution should be between 93.2°F and 98.6°F.

The crystal salt ionizer has been especially helpful for people with asthma because it binds dust particles and pollen, creating a seashore-like environment in the room. Furthermore, with the crystal salt ionizer we're not only getting pure air, but also a neutral frequency pattern in our room. Place the device in a location where you spend most of your time.

The ionizer does not have to be turned on permanently; it's sufficient to run the device for two to three hours at a time.

You can inhale the mist from the ionizer.

Bathe in a 1% *sole* solution once a week to relax and reduce the stress in your body.

Treat yourself to a floatation tank therapy. The high salt concentration in the tank creates a frequency pattern that boosts the body's energy and considerably supports the healing process.

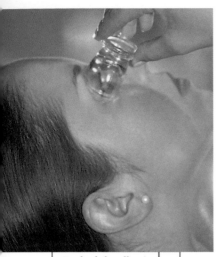

Eye bath for allergic conjunctivitis. See instructions on page 167

countries suffer from hay fever. With environmental pollution already overtaxing our body's ability to adapt, we have less immune protection against the increasingly aggressive pollen caused by air pollution. The first signs of hay fever are sneezing and itching of the nose and eyes, and the excreting of a watery solution by the nose.

Salt Applications for Hay Fever

Drink one teaspoon of *sole* in a glass of living spring water every morning on an empty stomach.

Drink two to three quarts of low mineral and non-carbonated water per day.

Flush your nose using a neti pot filled with 1% *sole* solution several times a day. The flushing removes the pollen adhering to your nose mucosa and regenerates the membrane.

If your eyes are affected, wash your eyes several times a day in 1% *sole* solution. Don't worry; the *sole* won't burn since it has the same salt concentration as your tear fluid.

A crystal salt ionizer would be of great help as well. The pollen, which is the cause of the problem, is bound in the *sole* mist and falls to the ground. This frees the air in your room from most of the pollen.

Colds

Colds, accompanied by coughing, runny nose, sore throat, bronchitis, sinus infections, eardrum infections and infectious flu, do not occur only during the cold and wet seasons, but all through the year, according to your disposition. Salt applications not only help to relieve the cold, but are also excellent preventive therapies.

Infectious Flu

Unlike the flu, the infectious flu is comparatively harmless, causing a general feeling of malady, inflammation of the upper respiratory tract, fever, headaches and growing pains.

Salt Applications for Infectious Flu

Drink one teaspoon of *sole* in a glass of living spring water every morning on an empty stomach.

Drink two to three quarts of low mineral and non-carbonated water per day.

If you are already experiencing the symptoms of the infection but do not have fever or just a slight increase in temperature, take a 1% *sole* bath in 98.6°F water for 20 minutes. Through osmosis, the body releases toxins and absorbs energy and minerals from the *sole*.

If you have a fever, *sole* bathing is not recommended.

Instead, soak your feet in a 1% *sole* solution and apply the salt shirt therapy.

Cold *sole* soaked thigh wraps are very effective for lowering fever.

Sore Throat

A sore throat is often the precursor of a cold. The throat feels scratchy, burns, and it hurts to swallow. The mouth is the most common gateway for infections to enter our body, and if the immune system is not strong enough, the throat and pharynx can get infected.

Salt Applications for Sore Throat

Drink one teaspoon of *sole* in a glass of living spring water every morning on an empty stomach.

Drink two to three quarts of low mineral and non-carbonated water per day.

Gargle with a 1% *sole* solution. This moisturizes the infected mucous membrane and loosens bacteria and viruses; the salt disinfects and regenerates the mucous membrane. Repeat this process several times a day.

A cold throat wrap with highly concentrated *sole* will alleviate the soreness. Soak a towel in pure sole, wrap it around your neck and, further, wrap a dry towel around that. Keep it around your neck for one hour.

Eardrum Infection

The swelling of the nose and throat area can lead to the closure of the ear trumpet, the pathway between the nose and the eardrum. This can result in a painful infection, as the air can no longer find its way to the eardrum, and mucous accumulates in the ear. This sets the condition for a variety of pathogens. The ear trumpet needs to be opened to allow for air circulation. Therefore, to treat the swelling in the nose area is as important as it is to treat the ear.

The heated salt sachet alleviates the pain in the ear. Apply the crystal sole peloid on the problem area.

Salt Applications for Eardrum Infection

Drink one teaspoon of *sole* in a glass of living spring water every morning on an empty stomach.

Drink two to three quarts of low mineral and non-carbonated water per day.

Flush your nose twice a day with a 1% *sole* solution.

To alleviate the pain in your ear, place the crystal salt sachet, heated to 120-140°F in the oven, on your ear for 20 minutes. Repeat several times a day.

Runny Nose and Sinus Infection

Runny or congested noses are not considered as illnesses per se. Nevertheless they have an impact on our well-being. There are some who suffer continually from chronic nose congestion. This condition can lead to sinus infections and headaches. If you currently suffer from these symptoms, you should make it a habit to flush your nose. The salt solution moisturizes the mucosa and supports its natural regeneration, making it more difficult for the bacteria and viruses to nest. Especially during the wintertime the dry heat from electric heaters and furnaces targets the mucosa. Use a neti pot for effectively cleaning the sinus at least twice daily as the infection persists.

Ideal for preventing runny or congested noses as well as sinus infections: the sole flush. See instructions on page 166

Salt Applications for a Runny or Congested Nose and Sinus Infection

Drink one teaspoon of *sole* in a glass of living spring water every morning on an empty stomach.

Drink two to three quarts of low mineral and non-carbonated water per day.

Flush your nose twice a day with a 1% *sole* solution.
This should become as habitual as brushing your teeth.

For sole inhalation instructions, see page 164

Bronchitis

Oftentimes a cold will follow a certain pattern: starting in the throat, rising to the nose and finally attacking the bronchi. Bronchitis manifests in different forms and can take up to several weeks to recede. Chronic bronchitis is especially found among smokers. The associated cough can be dry, spasmodic, or with phlegm. With phlegm, viruses, bacteria and pollutants are being expelled. It is especially important to drink lots of water with bronchitis to loosen the phlegm, making it easier to be expelled. Salt treatments will significantly support and accelerate the recovery process.

Salt Applications for Bronchitis

Drink one teaspoon of *sole* in a glass of living spring water every morning on an empty stomach.

Drink two to three quarts of low mineral and non-carbonated water per day.

Perform a *sole* inhalation therapy once or twice a day with a 1% *sole* solution. The *sole* concentration can be increased up to 3%.

For chronic bronchitis we recommend using a crystal salt ionizer.

Diseases of the Locomotion System

In this chapter we summarize all diseases that are related to our locomotion system such as infectious arthritis, degenerative arthritis, rheumatoid arthritis, rheumatic processes, gout, rheumatism of the fibrous tissues, osteoporosis, injuries, etc. With all rheumatic processes we can find re-crystallized deposits in the joints. The primary causes of rheumatic diseases are lack of exercise and water and poor nutrition over a long period of time. Contributing factors to a poor diet include: excessive consumption of

animal proteins, sugar, table salt, refined flours and alcohol. Coupled with the lack of water, the body is not able to flush the toxins from the system.

With all rheumatic illnesses the *sole* drinking therapy should be continued for a minimum of three months in order to hold this particular frequency pattern in the body. Slowly, the body starts to break down, metabolize and excrete the crystalline deposits in the joints. This process will initially aggravate the symptoms and pain. In order to minimize these effects, it is recommended to drink liberal quantities of good quality, living water that is low in minerals. Only this kind of water can support the body in removing the loosened toxins. The more water we drink the less pain we will experience during the initial aggravation of the symptoms. Floatation tank therapy brings great relief for rheumatic illnesses. However, it should be avoided during a rheumatic flare-up.

With rheumatic problems, it is especially important to drink liberal quantities of water to relieve the pain caused by the initial aggravation effects

211

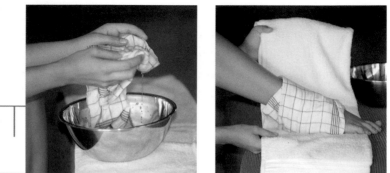

This is how you apply a sole wrap properly. See directions on page 176

Arthritis and Gout

Infectious rheumatic changes are characterized by painful swelling, heat and reddening of the skin, e.g., poly-arthritis or a gout attack. In this case warmth will increase the discomfort of the symptoms, whereas cold will have an alleviating effect.

Salt Applications for Arthritis and Gout

Drink one teaspoon of *sole* in a glass of living spring water every morning on an empty stomach.

Drink two to three quarts of low mineral and non-carbonated water per day.

If you desire a cooling effect, soak a towel in a cold, pure (26%), *sole* solution and wrap it around the affected area. Repeat several times daily.

The Water & Salt Peloid (*sole* mud) wrap will alleviate the pain as well. You can place a cold, wet towel over the sole mud to prevent it from drying out too quickly. Apply the wrap for one hour.

Arthrosis and Osteoporosis

The principal cause of degenerative rheumatic diseases such as rheumatoid arthritis and osteoporosis are deterioration of the cartilage and wearing of the tissues. Applying heat to the affected areas can alleviate the resulting pain. Osteoporosis patients especially benefit from the *sole* drinking therapy because it provides the body with all the minerals it needs in a form that the body can readily absorb and metabolize. Forget what you've been told about the calcium found in milk. Even though milk contains abundant calcium, it is of no use to our body because our system cannot break down cow's milk. If we want sufficient calcium in our diet, we need to eat nuts, whole wheat, sesame products and legumes. These foods contain amino acids in readily available forms.

The minerals in the crystal salt can be metabolized by the body and provide relief for osteoperosis

---

Salt Applications for Arthrosis and Osteoporosis

Drink one teaspoon of *sole* in a glass of living spring water every morning on an empty stomach.

Drink two to three quarts of low mineral and non-carbonated water per day.

Heat is good for all degenerative bone diseases. For the *sole* wraps, use warm water with a *sole* concentration of at least 10% or 3.2 ounce of salt to every 32 ounces of water.

Heat a crystal salt sachet to 120 - 140°F in the oven and place it on the problem area for 20 minutes.

Take a 2% *sole* bath (2 kilos of salt in 28 gallons of water) and gradually increase the concentration up to 8%.

▶

Salt applications in various forms

> Soak for 20 minutes. The water temperature should not exceed 98.6°F.
>
> Caution: do not take a *sole* bath in instances of acute rheumatic or gout flare-ups. In instances where the pain is localized in the joints of hands or feet, soak them in a higher *sole* concentration.
>
> Start with a concentration of 10% and slowly increase up to 20%. Again, the ideal temperature of 98.6°F guarantees a maximum exchange between the tissue fluid and the *sole*. Toxins can be eliminated and minerals and trace elements can be absorbed.
>
> Treat yourself to a floatation tank therapy session. (Avoid during a flare-up of condition.)

Broken Bones, Strained and Pulled Muscles or Tendons

Injuries of the locomotive system always cause inflammation and, therefore, are to be treated like infectious, rheumatic diseases. *Sole* not only alleviates the pain and reduces the

swelling, but also accelerates the regeneration of the injured tissue. Therefore, broken bones can especially benefit from *sole* therapy, because the minerals in the *sole* help to rebuild bones.

Salt Application for Injuries

Drink one teaspoon of *sole* in a glass of living spring water every morning on an empty stomach.

Drink two to three quarts of low mineral and non-carbonated water per day.

Wrap a towel soaked in a highly concentrated cold *sole* solution around the injured area and wrap a dry towel around it. It is recommended to repeat this process several times.

A Water & Salt Peloid (*sole* mud) wrap will also help. Place a cold, wet towel over the *sole* mud to prevent it from drying out too quickly. Keep the infected area wrapped for several hours.

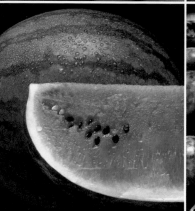

Indigestion and Malfunctioning Metabolism

The most common health related problems in the Western world are indigestion and rheumatic diseases. The causes are usually the same: lack of exercise, unhealthy life-style, poor nutrition, and lack of water. This leads to stomach trouble, diarrhea, constipation, liver and gallbladder problems, excess fat in the blood and urine, diabetes and intestinal putrefaction. With all the diseases mentioned above, the reasons for maintaining a healthy, balanced diet should be obvious. It is fundamental to every human being, for achieving and maintaining health. Basically, your diet should consist of natural, wholesome and living foods. Unnatural foods, such as white flower, sweets and canned foods should be avoided. You should lean more towards alkaline-forming foods in your diet. Most people have an acidic condition, the cause of many illnesses. Alkaline-forming foods include fruits, vegetables, greens and spelt. Acid-forming foods include all meats, sugar, eggs and dairy products. Nuts and plant-based oils are considered neutral. It is recommended to use high quality, cold-pressed, plant-based oils for cooking. With this habit you can even lower your cholesterol. A well-balanced diet consists of one-third acid-forming and two-thirds alkaline-forming foods. Remember to drink sufficient amounts of water: for every 2 lbs. of body weight, drink 1 oz. of good water (as mentioned above). This formula generally adds up to two to three quarts of water per day. If you implement the *sole* drinking therapy, your digestive problems should soon be history. The *sole* stimulates the peristalsis of your digestive organs, balances the stomach acid, supports the production of digestive fluids in the liver and pancreas, regulates the metabolism and harmonizes the acid-alkaline balance.

For every human being, a diet of living food is fundamental to achieving and maintaining health

Drink one teaspoon of *sole* in a glass of living spring water every morning on an empty stomach.

Drink two to three quarts of low mineral and non-carbonated water per day.

After several months of *sole* drinking therapy, gallstones may be broken down (if you have any) and passed through the urinary tract, which can sometimes be very painful.

In case of liver and gall bladder problems, or cramps in the stomach/intestine area, a warm *sole* wrap will alleviate the pain. Use 1 pint of very warm water and 1.8-3.5 oz of crystal salt. Soak a cotton towel in the *sole* solution and place it on the painful area. Place a dry towel over your belly and rest for 30 minutes.

Kidney and Bladder Problems

To maintain well-functioning kidneys, it is essential to drink liberal quantities of water

The kidneys are among our most important detoxification organs. They filter our blood while extracting pollutants. The urine flows from the kidneys through the ureter into the bladder and is passed on through the urethra. Women tend to suffer from urinary tract infections more often than men because the female urinary tract is only 0.9 inch long, a shorter journey for bacteria to travel. But men are seven times more likely than women to have kidney stones. To maintain well functioning kidneys, it is essential to drink liberal quantities of water: at least 1 ounce of good water for every 2 pounds of body weight. Most people not only drink insufficient quantities of water, but also the wrong kind of water. This leads to the accumulation of residues and toxins that cannot be properly disposed of, thereby damaging the kidneys. Support the proper functioning of your kidneys by drinking sufficient living water, low on minerals and non-carbonated. This is even more important if you are already suffering from kidney or bladder problems. The sole drinking therapy even breaks down and dissolves kidney and gallbladder stones. Passing the stones can sometimes be very painful. However, the endeavor will be worthwhile, as the body will have healed itself on its own. Please note: People suffering from renal insufficiency must not intake any quantities of salt. People with kidney disorders should consult their doctor first.

The rule of thumb is: Drink at least 1 ounce of water for every 2 pounds of body weight

Salt Applications for Kidney and Gallbladder Problems

Drink one teaspoon of *sole* in a glass of living spring water every morning on an empty stomach.

Drink two to three quarts of low mineral and non-carbonated water per day.

If you are experiencing pain in your kidney areas, use hot, moist, *sole* soaked wraps.

You can also use a heated crystal salt sachet on the painful area.

Cardiovascular Diseases

Sole is even capable of dissolving deposits in our blood vessels

Heart and circulatory diseases are the most common illnesses known to human beings. Every problem, from high and low blood pressures to the calcification of the blood vessels or coronary heart disease, can be linked to an unhealthy life-style: poor nutrition, lack of exercise, stress and cigarette smoking. But these destructive processes can be stopped by a radical change in our life-style, replacing bad habits with good ones. *Sole* therapy will greatly support this process. *Sole* therapy, over a longer period of time, is even capable of dissolving deposits in our blood vessels. It is absolutely essential to drink liberal quantities of good spring water so that these loosened deposits can be flushed out of your system. Otherwise they will circulate in your blood and the body will be forced to redeposit them. *Sole* has a balancing effect on blood pressure. Generally speaking, if the blood pressure is too low, *sole* can help to raise it, and vice versa.

(Caution: If you are among the 3% percent of people whose blood presure is sensitive to salt intake, you should use *sole* in drops only and consult your physician first.)

Salt Applications for Cardiovascular Diseases

Drink one teaspoon of *sole* in a glass of living spring water every morning on an empty stomach.

Drink two to three quarts of low mineral and non-carbonated water per day.

Treat yourself to a floatation tank therapy to experience the balancing effects on your body.

Nervousness, Poor Concentration, Sleeping Disorders

Many people today suffer from nervousness, an inability to concentrate and insomnia. Children with ADHD symptoms have been able to benefit from crystal salt lamps. A crystal lamp is ideal for small children, especially those who are afraid of sleeping in the dark and need a light source. The warm light has a very soothing effect and the salt's vibrations neutralize the damaging electromagnetic fields. It should be understood that computers and TVs do not belong, under any circumstances, in bedrooms or children's rooms. If you cannot avoid having a computer in the bedroom, at least make sure that there is no electrical current flowing to it while you sleep.

Crystal salt can neutralize damaging electromagnetic vibrations

Salt Applications for Nervous Disorders

Drink one teaspoon of *sole* in a glass of living spring water every morning on an empty stomach.

Drink two to three quarts of low mineral and non-carbonated water per day.

Treat your self to a *sole* bath every once in a while. A 1% *sole* solution in 98.6°F degrees water is sufficient. Try to forget your problems while you are relaxing in the tub, listening to some soothing music.

Treat yourself to a floatation tank therapy to recuperate and recharge yourself.

If you spend a lot of time in front of the computer, we recommend using a crystal salt ionizer to bind the excess positive ions that are causing damaging electro-smog. Within two hours the ionizer builds up a neutral vibration pattern in the room.

Crystal salt lamps also help to create a healthier electromagnetic atmosphere in the room.

Cancer

Cancer is understood to be an uncontrolled, destructive growth of degenerated cells. A cancer diagnosis is often interpreted as a death sentence. Cancer is synonymous with disorder and chaos in our body, caused by an energy deficit. The reasons for these energy deficits can be numerous and varied, for example, a genetic predisposition, poor nutrition or environmental influences. However, of great importance are the psychological factors, such as negative thoughts and emotions, lack of love in relationships and for your own self, life fears, constant internal stress or a stressful environment. All these factors destroy the natural frequency pattern in your body. At this point we will not claim that crystal salt can heal cancer. However, with the *sole* therapy you can, nevertheless, strengthen your energetic reserves to a great degree by replenishing the missing frequency pattern which will in turn, activate your body's self-healing abilities. If you remember, in the first chapter of the book we said that there is no such thing as an incurable disease. However, you must also do your part. You must radically change your perspective, your way of thinking. You must act positively! Like attracts like. Keep the company of positive people who appreciate you. Avoid negative stress. Eat healthy. Drink plenty of good water. With the crystal salt, give your body the missing frequency pattern and regain your full energy potential.

The frequency pattern of the crystal salt can strengthen your energy reserve

Salt Applications for Cancer

Drink one teaspoon of *sole* in a glass of living spring water every morning on an empty stomach.

Drink two to three quarts of low mineral and non-carbonated water per day.

Treat yourself to a *sole* bath, as often as your physical condition allows. A 1% *sole* solution in water of 98.6°F is sufficient.

Treat yourself to the profound experience of a floatation tank therapy.

Women's Health Issues

To be a woman nowadays means to adopt a variety of roles. Besides the classic images of a housewife, mother and loving partner, the woman of today also has to tackle jobs and contribute to the general financial support of the family. This multitasking requires a lot of energy and very often leads to chronic exhaustion. Womens health issues include ailments such as menstrual pains, PMS (pre-menstrual syndrome), abdominal pains, yeast infections, vaginal dryness, bacterial and viral infections, menopausal discomfort, and more. The salt kills bacteria, viruses and funguses and arrests their growth. The mucous membranes will become moist again and will rejuvenate, thus building up resistance against new infections.

Salt Applications for Womens Health Issues

Drink one teaspoon of *sole* in a glass of living spring water every morning on an empty stomach.

For problems with yeast infection, dry mucous membranes, or other vaginal infections, a *sole* bath for the lower half of your body is recommended. Choose a salt concentration between 3% and 8% in a 980F temperature water.

With a full body bath the initial concentration should not exceed 2%. It can be gradually increased up to 5%. Try to keep the bath water at or about body temperature of 980F.

Treat yourself to a floatation tank therapy to recuperate and recharge yourself.

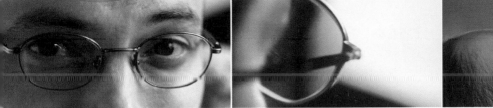

The 1% sole solution does not burn or sting your eyes because it equals the salt concentration of your tear fluid

Diseases of the Eye

Over sixty percent (60%) of the American population wear glasses as a result of congenital, impaired eyesight and old age. The latter occurs due to the dehydration of the eyeball. The most common problems, however, arise as a result of environmental factors. These include spending significant amounts of time in front of computer monitors or TV screens, forced-air from heaters, air conditioning units or furnaces and, of course, a deficiency of water in the body, which causes dry eyes. Pollen too can cause allergic reactions. *Sole* eye baths, when applied regularly over a long period of time, can alleviate these problems and even reduce impaired eye-sight due to old age. The salt binds the water, and the eyeball regains its natural form.

Salt Application for Diseases of the Eye

With an acute condition, wash your eyes with a 1% *sole* solution two to three times a day.

With a chronic condition, wash your eyes with a 1% *sole* solution twice to three times a day until the problem subsides.

Because the 1% *sole* solution equals the salt concentration of your tear fluids, this eye-bath will not burn or sting.

*It cannot be repeated often
enough: Drink
plenty of water to flush out
toxins in your system*

Heavy Metals

Many people have accumulated heavy metals in their body such as lead, cadmium, arsenic, palladium, amalgam or mercury, without knowing it. Our soils are polluted with these toxins, as are our teeth. They are a burden to our system because it is extremely difficult for our body to eliminate them. The consequences can include headaches, exhaustion, depression, loss of vitality and such. Crystal salt can help remove these toxins from our bodies.

Oral and Dental Hygiene

Crystal salt is excellent for oral and dental hygiene. It slows the formation of tartar and prevents cavities. Most dental decay is caused by overly acid mouth and throat flora. Even in instances where tartar is present, *sole* can remove it. The crystal salt brings your mouth flora back into a neutral, balanced state and will heal existing illnesses, rot or decay and prevent future

---

Salt Application for Heavy Metals

Drink one teaspoon of *sole* in a glass of water every day on an empty stomach. It is important to drink plenty of good water that is low in minerals throughout the day. In this way your body can quickly flush the dislodged, ionized and metabolized heavy metals before they can be re-circulated through your system.

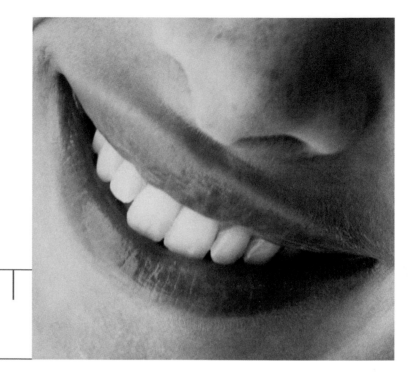

Healthy teeth and healthy gums not only add beauty, but are also important to our health

Rinsing you mouth with concentrated *sole* can remove tartar and prevent tooth decay

occurrences. It also helps to protect and help regenerate the enamel. Hildegard von Bingen, the German mystic we mentioned earlier in this book, recommended using salt for dental hygiene and to prevent bleeding gums.

Salt Application for Oral and Dental Hygiene

Brush your teeth every morning with a *sole* concentration of 10 to 26%. Use a *sole* with the same concentration to gargle in the morning. Swish it around in your mouth for three minutes before spitting it out.

Salt-Based Skin & Body Care and Wellness

Crystal salt has not only proven itself in the medical field but also in the arenas of beauty and skin care. Not so long ago, salt-based beauty and skin care products were rare. But recently, the skin and beauty care industries have re-discovered the benefits of salt. Today we can find numerous salt-based beauty products on the shelves of food stores and drugstores alike, ranging from soaps and lotions to masks and peelings and even hair care products. However, most of the products you find in stores are still produced with refined salts. Now, we would like to introduce you to two crystal salt products that have applications for both skin care and therapeutic benefit.

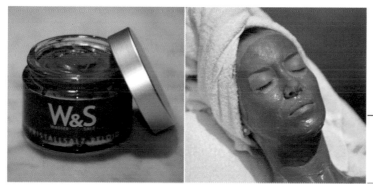

The Water&Salt Peloid mask regenerates the skin and prevents wrinkling

Rejuvenate Your Skin with the Water & Salt Peloid Mask

Apply the Water&Salt Peloid mask once a week to revitalize your skin. The rejuvenating properties of the crystal *sole* binds fluids in the skin layers, tightens the skin and makes wrinkles disappear. Regular use can prevent new wrinkles from appearing. Skin impurities are neutralized and the skin is naturally regenerated. The best results can be experienced after a sauna, when your pores are wide open, or after a steam bath.

Natural Deodorant

Salt is a natural deodorant. Through its disinfecting and neutralizing effects it prevents the forming of germs and bacteria that
cause unpleasant body odor, when the body is not alkaline.
Germs and bacteria can germinate quickly in an overly acid environment. Take a stone of crystal salt, lightly moisten it with
water and apply it as you would any under-arm deodorant.

Regeneration Through Whole-Body Peeling

Are you battling fatigue and low energy? Then why not treat yourself to a whole-body peeling? The peeling is ideal after using the sauna. If you cannot go to a sauna then at least take a hot shower beforehand to open your pores. Lie on a large linen cloth or towel and lavishly apply the Water&Salt Peeling to your whole body. (Or prepare a mixture of crystal salt and a natural oil; comp. p. 177.) Wrap yourself in the towel or linen cloth and additionally a warm blanket. Lie down and relax for 30-40 minutes. After some time you will feel pleasurable warmth rising in your body. Now, every cell in your body is activated to its fullest potential. During this time your body will undergo a significant detoxification. At the same time you will receive an enormous energy infusion, caused by the highly concentrated crystal salt mixture. The body will shed its dead skin and the skin cells will be replenished and moisturized again. The circulation of blood through the skin increases, causing the skin to tighten and become firm. After 30-40 minutes gently shower the peeling off with lukewarm water. Gently pat your skin dry. Do not rub. The oil will remain on your skin leaving it smooth and velvety.

The crystal salt peeling removes dead skin and replenishes and moisturizes the skin cells

231

In

Conclusion

Expand your Consciousness

At this point let us recall one of the prophecies of the Native Americans. About 350 years ago, they predicted that there would be a time when our plates would be full yet we would have nothing to eat. The Native Americans refer to this as the "quiet or passive war," as they themselves remain as passive observers. The prophecy further reveals that the white man need not be challenged to engage in war, but that he will annihilate himself. This "slow suicide" is happening throughout the modern industrialized world. Without recognizing the true value of nutrition as a life giving force, we simply stuff ourselves without consideration. We consume great quantities of "processed material" wrongly thinking it to be food. But our bodies continue to be hungry because the so-called food we are giving it does not contain the correct information. This kind of behavior has turned us into consumers rather than customers. Customers know their needs and how to satisfy them whereas a consumer's needs are dictated by advertisers. Consumption only creates unhappiness. Those who are unhappy will constantly look for satisfaction, becoming driven by their need for more. Meanwhile, the advertisements and commercials add fuel to the fire by telling us every day that we're lacking something and that they can give us just what we need to become satisfied. We continue to search for happiness in the material (consumer) world, but, unfortunately, will never be able to find it. We try to fill the emptiness within ourselves through quick satisfaction, by consuming

Regretfully, many customers have become consumers, trying to find fulfillment in shopping malls

something. This will numb the empty feeling for a moment but will never be able to genuinely satisfy it. In return, we become addicted because it leaves us wanting more. We become slaves to the desires that have been created by the industry for profits, and we dive into the frantic game of consumerism for a false sense of security from the accumulation of material things, most of which we don't even need.

Time for a New Beginning

Maybe you are asking yourself why our society has become so degraded and what we, as individuals, can do against the negative, materialistic industries, politics and sciences. We always have a tendency to blame others. But the true answer can only be found within ourselves. We cannot blame others for turning us into helpless slaves. It always takes two to play the game – one who acts and one who accepts the action. The real one to blame will never be found outside, but deep within our own self. Our whole life is based on polarity and works as a mirror. As long as there are people who demand that their doctors treat their headache symptoms, there will always be doctors, according to the law of polarity, who will write them prescriptions. Therefore, the doctors are not to be blamed, it is we who are responsible.

Raise your Consciousness

Once we raise our consciousness, our actions will automatically change, causing a change in everything around us. We may not like the world the way it is, but remember, it was we who made it this way. Everything is only a question of consciousness. If we change from within, our perspective and our actions will resonate this change, and the world around us will respond. The good news is – it is never too late to start! Let us regain a sense for true quality of life. Recognize how all things are interconnected. Become aware of how free you can be, simply by expanding your consciousness. Remember, energy can be changed at any given moment, even matter. After having survived your first detoxification phase, you will be surprised to discover a new feeling for a life worth living. Rediscover and strive for your ideals. Find a new sense of purpose for your life. Set goals for yourself and attain them. Follow your inner voice and discover your life's real calling, to realize your true self. Only then will you become truly free and independent.

Discover Holism

To understand that there is a natural interrelation and interconnection among all things is not as complicated as it appears to be. It's quite the opposite. The principal order of nature, in its holistic form, is actually very simple to comprehend. Support those people around you who are trying, with their idealism, to make this world a better place. Become an idealist yourself, and recognize that all things are connected, from the infinitely small to the infinitely large. Nature will never deceive us. We, as human beings, are small cells in the bigger body of Earth, which in turn is a small cell in the bigger body of the universe. From a holistic perspective, we are able to see which vital role each and every one of us plays and contributes. At this point, let's stop and think about the true purpose of our life. Are we really born on this planet destined only to work? Is it possible that the purpose of our life, from the beginning to this moment, is a continual developing process? The path to self-awareness is the goal; and, according to the law of cause and effect, everyone is destined to walk this path. Some take the direct route while others meander. However the goal will always be the same: to raise our consciousness to attain "all-consciousness," to become Cryst-al.

Discover Holism; raise your consciousness; become Cryst-al

Water Literature:

Alexandersson, Olof: Lebendes Wasser, Ennsthaler Verlag 1998, ISBN 3-85068-377-X

Buchman, Dian: The Complete Book of Water Healing, Instant Improvement 1998, ISBN 0-941683-33-8

Dalla Via, Gudrun: Phänomen Wasser, VGS Verlag 1997, ISBN 3-8025-1332-0

Emoto, Masuro: The Message from Water, Hado Kyoikusha, Tokyo 2001

Engler, Ivan: Wasser – Polaritätsphänomen, Deutscher Sparbuchverlag 1999, ISBN 3-88778-227-5

Flanagan, Patrick: Elixier der Jugendlichkeit, Waldthausen Verlag 1994, ISBN 3-926453-67-2

Heininger, Franz: Trinkwasser – Ernähre dich bewusst, Ennsthaler Verlag 1998, ISBN 3-85068-552-7

Hendel, Barbara : Wasser vom Reinsten, Ina Verlag 2002, ISBN 3-9808408-1-6

Honauer, Urs: Wasser – die geheimnisvolle Energie, Irisiana Verlag 1998, ISBN 3-89631-240-5

Ryrie, Charlie: Heilende Energie des Wassers, Urania Verlag 1999, ISBN 3-908652-01-4

Schwenk, Theodor: Das sensible Chaos, Verlag freies Geistleben 1995, ISBN 3-7725-0571-6

Salt Literature: (most was written in regard to chemical composition, but will be helpful sometimes)

Braunschweig-Pauli, Dagmar: Jod-Krank, Dingfelder Verlag 2000, ISBN 3-926253-58-4

Brezenski, Gerald: Grenzflächen & Kolloide, ISBN 3860250167

Brucker Dr., M.O.: Störungen der Schilddrüse, Emu Verlag 1996, ISBN 3-89189-062-1

Falckenberg, Saskia: Salz ist Leben, Ariston Verlag 1987, ISBN 3-7205-1462-5

Geerlings, Jürgen: Bestimmung der Aktivitätskoeffizienten von Salz-Wasser Mischungen über den gesamten Konzentrationsbereich, Shaker Verlag, ISBN 3826544285, ISBN 3-517-01597-0

Joly, Dominique: Woher kommt das Salz, ISBN 3473383384

Kirchgessner, Manfred: Spurenelemente und Ernährung, ISBN 3804710956

Krahe, Michael: Kristallklar, Osterholz Verlag, ISBN 3-9804503-3-3

Neumeister, Andreas: Salz im Blut, ISBN 351840220X

Rosenstock, Celia: Salz – Der Ratgeber für Gesundheit, Verlag Brasil Mineracao 1998, ISBN 3-9806554-0-7

Schleimer, Jochen: Salze des Lebens, Sonntag Verlag 1997, ISBN 3-87758-135-8

Schweiger, Anita: Heilen mit Salz, Verlag Knaur 2000, ISBN 3-426-87042-8

Seldin and Giebisch: The Regulation of Sodium Chloride Balance, ISBN 0881674818

Steiner, Gertraud: Salz als Attraktion, ISBN 3701309698

Unterricht Chemie: 17 Bände, Band 4 - Salze, ISBN 3761415591

Wormer, Eberhard: Die Heilkraft des Salzes, Südwest Verlag 1995,

English Literature:

Adrogue, Horacio: Salt & Water – 532 formidable questions, ISBN 0865424268

Batmanghelidj, F. M.D.: Your Body's Many Cries for Water, ISBN 0-9629942-3-5

Biser, Sam: How to Heal Disease with Salt

Dewan, A.P.: Food For Health, A C Specialist Publishers Pvt Ldt., New Delhi, India

Kaufmann, Klaus: Sodium Chloride, ISBN 00657719

Kaufmann, Klaus: Silica – The Amazing Gel, Alive Books, Vancouver, Canada, ISBN 0-920470-30-0

Multhauf, R.: Neptune's Gift, UMI Books on Demand

Robbins, John: Diet for a New America, ISBN 1574355064

Schulkin, Jay: Sodium Hunger – The Search for a Salty Taste, ISBN 0521353688

Literature: Biophysics – Biochemistry – Science – Holism:

Bischof, Marco: Biophotonen – Das Licht in unseren Zellen, Verlag Zweitausendeins 1999, ISBN 3-861150-095-7

Coats, Callum: Naturenergien verstehen und nutzen, Omega Verlag 1999, ISBN 3-930243-14-8

Dahlke, Rüdiger: Wege der Reinigung, Bertelsmann Verlag 1998, Buch Nummer: 05072-4

Dethlefsen, Thorwald: Krankheit als Weg, Bertelsmann Verlag 1987, ISBN 3-570-03579-4

Dethlefsen, Thorwald. Schicksal als Chance, Arkana Verlag 1979, ISBN 3-442-11723-2

Ewert, K. D.: Das System der Angst, Ewert Verlag 2000, ISBN 3-89478-735-X

Hannemann, Holger: Energie Medizin, Ariston Verlag 1995, ISBN 3-7205-1841-8

Hendel, Barbara: Endlich frei von Allergie, Mosaik-Verlag München, 1999

Hopfner, Otto: Einhandrute und Pyramidenenergie, Silberschnur Verlag 1996, ISBN 3-931-652-05-X

Jasmuheen: In Resonanz – Das Geheimnis der richtigen Schwingung, Koha Verlag 2000, ISBN 3-929512-28-9

Jasmuheen: Lichtnahrung – Die Nahrungsquelle für das kommende Jahrtausend, Koha Verlag 2000, ISBN 3-929512-35-1

Jentschura, Peter: Gesundheit durch Entschlackung, Verlag Peter Jentschura 2001, ISBN 3-933874-33-5

Jürgenson, Johannes: Die lukrativen Lügen der Wissenschaft, Ewert Verlag 1998, ISBN 3-89478-699-X

Kohler, Bodo: Biophysikalische Informationstherapie, Fischer Verlag 1997, ISBN 3-437-55220-1

Langbein, Kurt: Gesunde Geschäfte – Die Praktiken der Pharmaindustrie, Verlag Kiepenheuer & Witsch 1983, ISBN 3-462-01549-4

Liberman, Jacob: Die heilende Kraft des Lichts, Verlag Piper 1998, ISBN 3-492-22005-3

Liekens, Paul: Das Geheimnis der Pyramidenenergie, Windpferd Verlag 1998, ISBN 3-89385-018-X

Lorber, Jakob: Die Heilkraft des Sonnenlichts, Lorber Verlag 1996, ISBN 3-87495-175-8

Ludwig Dr., Wolfgang: Informative Medizin, VGM Verlag 1999, ISBN 3-88699-050-8

Peters, Ralph: Das Pyramidenhandbuch, Weltenhüter Verlag 1997, ISBN 3-929681-61-7

Popp Prof. Fritz-Albert: Die Botschaft der Nahrung, Verlag Zweitausendeins 1999

Sander, Friedrich: Der Säure-Basenhaushalt des menschlichen Organismus, Hippokrates Verlag 1999, ISBN 3-7773-1428-5

Schmidt, Paul: Symphonie der Lebenskräfte, Paul Schmidt Verlag 1986

Steiner, Rudolf: Makrokosmos und Mikrokosmos, Rudolf Steiner Verlag 1992, ISBN 3-7274-7030-5

Toth, Max: Pyramid Power – Kosmische Energie der Pyramiden, Bauer Verlag 1999, ISBN 3-7626-0718-4

Wandmaker, Helmut: Rohkost statt Feuerkost, Waldthausen Verlag 1996, ISBN 3-442-13912-0

Wandmaker, Helmut: Willst Du Gesund sein? – Vergiss den Kochtopf, Waldthausen Verlag 1989, ISBN 3-926453-04-4

Product Suppliers

Information About:

- Original Himalayan Crystal Salt Products
- Water&Salt Documentary Film
  on DVD or VHS
- Water&Salt Skin & Body Care Products
- Distribution
- Sourcing

North America

Exclusively imported by:
American BlueGreen, LLC
Toll Free Tel.: 1 877-224-4872
www.americanbluegreen.com
email: info@americanbluegreen.com

United Kingdom

Best Care Products, LTD
Tel.: 01342 410 303
www.bestcare-uk.com
email: info@bestcare-uk.com

Australia

BioNatural Pty. Ltd
Toll Free Tel.: 1300 555 686
www.BioNatural.com.au
www.BioNatural.biz

Information About:

- Applications
- Science
- Ordering the Water&Salt Magazine
- AS List of Doctors and Therapists
- Membership

Water&Salt Association

P.O. Box 190
Umpqua, OR 97486
email: info@waterandsalt.us
www.waterandsalt.us

Information about Floatation Tanks and Locations:

www.floatation.com
www.samadhitank.com
www.floatdreams.com
Looking for a place to float anywhere in the world? Visit www.floatguide.com

Information about FIJI Water

Toll Free Tel.: 1 877-H2O-FIJI
(877-426-3454)
www.fijiwater.com

Personal Dedications

Peter Ferreira

I would like to dedicate this book with special thanks to all the kind people who have contributed to the creation of this book and supported me for all these years, either directly or indirectly; to my wife Mercedes and my children Marco and Natasha, for their patience and awareness, to my parents Fritz und Ilse for their holistic, wise approach in raising me and for helping me to become the independent person that I am; to my sister Elke and my brothers, Günter and Werner; as well as to Wilfried Geib, Klaus Wezyk, Bernd Nieswand, Wolf von Eberstein, Ron Lichtman and numerous kind friends for trusting in me.

Dr. Barbara Hendel

I dedicate this book to all of my past, present and future patients, who have the wisdom and awareness of approaching their healing process holistically. Every single patient has, through his personal story, contributed to my knowledge of the natural interconnectedness. I also want to thank all the people who have supported me in many ways throughout the creation of this book.

Imprint

Gymona Holding AG, Switzerland,
Copyright © 2002

Exclusive Rights worldwide for the English Edition:
Natural Resources, Inc., USA

Master Distributor:
Institute for Profound Living
www.profoundliving.org

Second English Edition:
50,000 copies printed

Graphic and Layout:
dworak & kornmesser, Germany

ISBN 0-9744515-1-7

Picture Credits

Dr. Masuro Emoto: P. 53, 54(3), 55(2)

Martin Kornmesser: (ESA-lnformation Centre): P. 8, 9, 233, 232

NASA & ESA: P. 14, 172

Peter Ferreira: P. 201, 202

Wolfgang Heisler: Cover (1), P. 12, 18(2), 26, 62, 72(2), 78, 160 (4), 163(2), 164, 166, 167(3), 175(2), 176, 178 (2), 179,180, 181, 182, 183, 192, 195, 196 (2), 204, 208, 209, 210, 212, 214 (3), 215 (2), 199, 225, 229 (2), 230 (2)

Dr. Wilhelm Höfer: P. 137 (3), 138 (3), 139 (3)

Prof. Manfred Karge: P. 139 (2)

Ruth Kübler: P. 140 (2)

Heidemaria Schornsteiner: Inner cover front - diagrams IMEDIS (6)

dworak & kornmesser: Cover (1), P. 1, 3, 8, 15, 32 (2), 51 (3), 96 (2), 98, 100 (2), 103, 105, 108, 124, 127, 144, 186, 188, 231, 232

elektravision: P. 2, 144, 149 (2)

image 100LTD: P. 6 (2), 155, 186, 197, 230,

Photo Disk: Cover: (2), P. 1, 2 (5), 3 (2), 8 (2), 12 (3), 16 (2), 17 (2), 19, 20, 23, 25 (3), 30, 32, 35, 40 (2), 41 (2), 42, 44 (2), 46, 49 (2), 50, 52, 56, 58, 60 (2) 61, 68, 96 (2), 100, 101 (2), 112, 114, 116, 144, 146, 148 (2), 149, 150, 151, 152, 170, 186 (2), 190 (3), 191 (3), 194, 200 (3), 201 (3), 216 (8), 225 (2), 233

PhotoAlto: Cover: (1), P. 1, 3, 36, 42, 44, 48, 66, 186, 188, 205, 206 (4), 220, 226, 228

FIJI Water photos courtesy of FIJI Natural Artesian Water: P. 80, 81 (4), 82, 83, 84 (2), 85, 86

Yaqara Valley photo courtesy of Three Loose Coconuts: P. 80 (1)

Internarional Institute of Biophysics: P 133 (2)

Special Note

Water and salt are the most elementary nutrients for the maintenance of the human body. In respect to certain laws, we would like to note that this book is dedicated towards the maintenance of health. Whosoever chooses to apply any of the suggestions mentioned in this book is responsible for their own actions. The authors and the publisher do not intend to state any diagnosis or suggest any form of therapy. The described applications are not to be substituted for professional medical treatment in case of illness or disease. All applications mentioned in the book using water and salt are supported by numerous scientific studies and sound research. However, the authors are not intending to give any medical advice.

The interested reader is neither directly nor indirectly engaged nor being recommended to renounce medical advice or medication. It is the sole intention of the authors to convey the biophysical insights of the abilities and properties of water and salt for a general well being. This book is meant to contribute to the understanding of natural, holistic connections. However, it is not meant to substitute fundamental medical advise of a doctor. We invite the interested reader to inform their doctors about the contents of this book. Applications of the therapies mentioned in this book are at the reader's own risk.

Glossary

Acid-alkaline balance: For our metabolism to function must maintain a certain acid-alkaline balance. Extreme acidity can lead to death. The acid-alkaline balance is mainly influenced by our diet; how much acid or alkaline forming foods we eat.

Anomaly: The prefix a(n) stands for "not." An anomaly is something ab-normal in a scientific sense, an irregularity.

Artesian spring: Water that surfaces on its own, due to levitational forces.

Alkaline: Term that describes a certain pH factor. The pH factor stands for a concentration of hydrogen ions. The more hydrogen ions present, the more acidic the condition. The pH scale reaches from 1 (= very acidic) to 14 (= very alkaline). Pure water has a pH value around 7 and is neutral. Our blood has a pH value of 7.35 (compare also acid-alkaline balance).

Biochemistry: A branch of chemistry studying the chemical behavior in living beings. Biochemistry is not only interested in the individual chemical components but in their vital interplay.

Biophysics: The science of living physics. This form of physics applies the knowledge of physics to explain biological questions, such as the transmission of nervous impulses or muscle control. The boundaries to biochemistry are in part, fluid, not solid.

Centrifugal: "Outward." Describes an apparent force that acts outward on a body moving about a center.

Centripetal: "Inward." Describes an apparent movement or tendency to move toward a center, inward from without.

Colloidal: Condition of matter depicted by its even distribution (solution) of microscopic particles with a diameter of 1 to 100 nm in a dispersing substance. Minerals are present in plants in colloidal form.

Colon-hydrotherapy: Modern form of cleansing the colon; flushing it with warm water or sole solution.

Cluster: Chemical term describing hydrogen bridges between molecules.

Crystal salt: The purest, natural form of salt, containing within its crystalline structure all elements and trace elements of which our body is consisting. Also called "halite."

Dehydrate: Losing water in the body, drying out. To absolutely or relatively lack water in the external or internal cellular space. In chemistry: to break apart hydrogen from its organic compounds.

Dipole: Chemical compounds with an unequally distributed electric charge, such as the water molecule: the oxygen atom is of negative charge and the two hydrogen atoms are of positive charge. Dipolar molecules mutually attract each other. This is how water molecules connect into clusters via hydrogen bridges.

Disharmony: Opposite of harmony, "un-sound," incoherent. The Latin prefix "dis" stands for "apart," "gone."

Dissonance: Occurs when vibrations of different wavelengths meet, which creates a state of chaos. Waves that vibrate at the same length create resonance. Literally dissonance means "un-sound".

Electronic acupuncture: A painless measurement method to diagnose and therapeutically alleviate dysfunctions in the body. Reveals smallest distortions of the organs. Allows for early diagnosis, before a disease materializes. It measures the skin resistance to find out the energetic potentials of the acupuncture points, which gives an accurate picture of the bio-energetic condition of the respective organ.

Electromagnetic magnetism: Created by electric current. Electromagnetic waves vibrate evenly and can expand in a vacuum. Electromagnetic fields transport electric as well as magnetic energy. They play an important role in regulating bodily functions.

Enzymes: Proteins that enable certain biological functions. Enzymes are catalysts: they can accelerate processes in our body without changing their form. They are essential for various bodily functions, such as digestion and blood coagulation. The lack of certain enzymes can lead to health problems and unbalance the metabolism.

Entropy (physics): Measure of disorganization or degradation in the universe that reduces available energy, or tendency of available energy to dwindle. Chaos, opposite of order.

Faraday cage: A metal shield, protecting its inner area from outer electric fields.

Free radicals: Molecules containing oxygen that attack cells in the body.

Frequency: Describes how often a wave repeats its vibration within a certain period of time, measured in Hertz.

Fungicide: Substance that kills fungi.

Gravitation/gravitational: Attractive force of Earth which causes all bodies in her atmosphere to move towards her center.

H2O: Chemical formula for water: two hydrogen atoms (=H) are connected with one oxygen atom (=O) in one water molecule.

Hertz: Measurement unit for vibrations or frequencies (certain amount of vibration in a certain period of time). One Hertz (Hz) equals one vibration per second. Light waves vibrate at several trillion Hertz. Sound waves, audible to the human ear, vibrate at a rate between 20 and 20,000 Hertz.

Hexagonal: Polygon having six angles and six sides.

Homeopathy: Medicine developed by Samuel Hahnemann towards the end of the 18th century, based on the understanding that healing comes from within, from the body's innate self-healing forces. These forces are to be stimulated by certain substances that would actually cause respective disease if given in a high doses; intending to heal an illness with its equal substance.

Homeostasis: Natural regulatory mechanism of the organism. Ability of the body to maintain its perfect, natural balance (e.g. the circulatory system, its temperature or its water and hormone balance). The hypothalamus is the central navigation system in the middle brain.

Hydrogen Bridges: Hydrogen atoms that create a connection between molecules/clusters.

Hydrotherapy: Water application therapy developed by Parson Kneipp, such as showers, baths or wraps. The Greek term for water is "hydro."

Implosive: Opposite of explosive. When forces condense towards the inside they create an energy that is directed inward, which reduces the volume and the temperature. This releases 127 times more energy than an explosion.

Intestinal flora: The sum of all bacteria and fungi that live in the intestine. A healthy intestinal flora supports the breaking down of nutrients, trains the immune system in the intestines, fights off pathogens and helps the body build the vitamins E and K. An unbalanced intestinal flora (e.g. when there are too many fungi or too little beneficial bacteria) can lead to many health problems.

Ions/ionized: Electrically charged atoms or atom groups. Ionization is the process in which an electrically charged atom or atom group absorbs or releases a negatively charged electron. This reaction can be stimulated. Ionizers are used to decalcify or energize water.

Isotone fluids: Fluids that have equal osmotic pressure. The Greek prefix "iso" means equal.

Levitation/levitational: Absence of gravitation, lifting. Possible through strong electromagnetic forces.

Low frequency range: Depicts electromagnetic fields of low frequency ranges down to 30 Kilohertz (kHz). The entire public production of electricity lies within the low frequency range.

Macrocosm: Outer space, universe. The Greek term "macro" stands for "big."

Meander, meander form: Depicts a winding water current. Meander means "twisting, winding, wavy." The spiraling movement of water is also-called the meander movement; blood and lymph (water in the tissue) also flow through our body in meandering fashion.

Manifest: To take form and become visible.

Metaphysical: Literally, beyond the physical realm, beyond that which we can realize or discover with our five senses. Also, a branch of philosophy which studies the "beingness" or inherent nature of reality.

Microcosm: In contrast to macrocosm, the universe of the smallest parts, atoms and even smaller phenomena. The Greek word "micro" means "small," "fine."

Molecule: Compound of two or more atoms, the smallest units of chemical compounds.

NaCl: Chemical formula for sodium chloride, industrially produced table salt.

Nanometer: Measuring unit, equaling 10 to the -9th meter, or 0.000000001 meter..

Non-organic: Not alive, the opposite of organic. Describes substances that do not derive from organic nature, such as minerals in stones.

Organic: In chemistry, the area which studies carbon compounds. In general, that which is alive, pertaining to a living organism.

Organometry: Every biological system has a complex regulatory mechanism which adapts to and protects against the changing environment. Organometry can determine these processes by diagnosing the circle diagrams of the meridians as well as by estimating the dynamic altering factors.

Osmosis: Transmission of fluids from one cell into another; foundation of metabolism, led by the concentration of salt within a cell. Water can penetrate cell membranes, and strives to, where the concentration of salt is highest, in order to equalize the salt concentration in the body.

Ozonation: Ozone treatment, e.g., to kill germs in water. Ozone is a very unstable and reactive gas similar to oxygen in its chemical structure; its molecule is made of three oxygen atoms.

Pasteurization: Flash heating of sensitive fluids such as milk, to kill bacteria. Pasteurized milk keeps longer. The pasteurizing process destroys the biophysical structure of milk.

Peloid: Natural, re-crystallized mineral mud. Crystal sole peloid is made of micro-mineral mud mixed with crystal sole.

Photon(s): Light particles, compound of tiny elementary particles, electromagnetic radiation. The measuring unit of photons are light quanta.

Photosynthesis: A process in which green plants create glucose and starch from sunlight, water and carbon dioxide, creating food for the plant and emitting oxygen. Essential process that enables life on Earth.

Piezo-electricity: Electrical tension created by pressure or expansion, found in specific crystals. The name comes from the Greek term "piezein" for "pushing" or "pressing."

Platonic bodies (aka sacred geometry): Geometric term, describing the three dimensional bodies with several sides which are all equal in size. There are 5 platonic bodies, their names deriving from the number of their sides: tetrahedron (four triangles), hexagon/cube (six squares), octahedron (eight triangles), dodecahedron (twelve pentagons), icosahedron (twenty triangles).

Polarity/polar: The opposition between two poles, such as between negatively and positively charged poles or between "good" and "bad," "yes" and "no." Polar thinking is thinking in black and white instead of allowing a full spectrum of color.

Principle order: Order that corresponds to the original geometric structure and vibration within our bodies describing the perfect balance of forces which maintain health.

Refined: Biophysical or chemical alteration of raw material. In regard to food, it means that components are removed in order to preserve them, destroying their holistic structure and energy/information/consciousness content.

Resonance: Literally means "to vibrate with." From the point of view of physics, resonance happens when two systems are vibrating within the same frequency range. When resonant waves meet, they create order. In contrast, when two waves vibrating at different frequencies meet, they create chaos or dissonance.

Rock salt: Original salt that has not yet obtained a crystalline structure. The minerals in the stone salt are too coarse to enter our cells.

Segmentary diagnostics: Measurement of biologically active zones with constant electric current of positive and negative charge (11uA, 1.24 V), followed by stimulation of these zones with electric impulses between 13 and 30 Hz. Segmentary diagnostics measures the interactions between the organs and their nervous supplies. The results are interpreted through integral and differential diagnosis.

Sole ("So-lay"): Water and salt solution. "Sol" is Latin for "salt" and "sun."

Synthetic: Not natural, artificial, man-made.

Toxic: Poisonous

Vibration pattern: The even pattern of electromagnetic waves within a certain period of time, also referred to as frequency.

Wavelength; Generally the distance from one wave peak to another. In electricity the wavelength describes the specific vibrational pattern of the current.

Index

A

Acid forming foods 40

Acid-alkaline balance 40

Acidic 40

Acne 189, 190

Addictions 159

Aggravation 211

Aging 190

Alkaline foods 40

Allergies 18, 200

Aluminum 114

Alzheimer 114

Amino acids 148, 213

Artesian 71, 72, 73, 79, 80, 82, 95

Arthritis 212. 213

Asthma 202, 203

Athletes foot 197, 198

B

Bach flower 49

Batmanehelidj, Farldum

Berchtesdgaden 119, 121, 122, 127

Beta-endorphines 174

Bingen, Hildegard von

Biophotons 132

   algae research 132

Bladder 90, 184, 218

Blood 92, 108, 115, 242

Blood circulation 90, 173

Blood pressure, high 92

Body peeling 178, 179

Body temperature 224

Bone diseases 212

Bronchitis 210

C

Calcium 19, 37, 40, 109, 115

Cancer 17, 114, 222, 223

Carbonated 47, 71, 72, 73, 74

Cardiovascular diseases 220

Carrel, Alexis 57

Cavities 228

Cheops pyramid 30

Chloride 146

Chlorine 69

Cholesterol 92, 217

Clusters 87

Coarse 74, 117, 165, 179

Codex Alimentarius 123

Cold, infectious

Colds 205

Colon cleanse 62

Colon hydrotherapy 62

Concentration, poor 221

Constipation 217

Coronary heart disease 220

Cosmetics 229

Cosmic order 31

Cough 205, 210

Crystal salt analysis 136

Crystal salt 98

Crystal salt ionizer 183

Crystal salt lamps 184

Crystal salt peloid 181

Crystalline structure 50

Crystals 27

D

Dehydration 225

Deposits 187

Depression 227

Diabetes 217

Diarrhea 217

Digestion 217

Distilled water 76

E

Ear infections 178

Eardrum infection 207

Earth-grid-net 86

Eczema 190

Egyptians 29

Electromagnetic fields 31, 59

Electromagnetic frequency patterns 59

Electronic acupuncture 17. 18

Electrons 22

Elements 99

Emoto, Dr. Masaru 53

Energetic vibrations 53

Energizing water 77

Energy 20, 31

Energy, deficit 17, 33

Energy matrix 97

Entropy 52

Evolution 9

Exhaustion 224

Eye bath 167

Eye, illnesses of 204

F

Facial mask 181

Fatima 64

Fever 206

FIJI Water 81-95

Floatation tank 171

Fluoride 69

Food 36, 39, 53

Food, dead 37, 53

Foot bath 62

Free radicals 184

Frugivore 70

Fungicides 67

G

Gallstones 110

Gemstone essences 49

Gorleben 128

Gout 110

Gravitational 57

H

Halite 118

Halogens 113

Hay fever 204

Headache 227

Healing water 71

Heart attack 155

Heavy metals 227

Herpes 175

Himalayan crystal salt 120

Hoefer, Dr. Wilhelm 136

Homeopathy 49

Homeostasis 10, 33, 35

Hydrotherapy 61

I

IMEDIS 90, 130

Injury 211

Insect bites 174

Institute for Biophysical Research 129

Iodine 113

J

Joints, ailments of the 176

K

Kage, Prof. Manfred 138

Kidney and bladder diseases 217

Kidney stones 111

Kneipp, Sabastian 61

Kübler, Ruth 140

L

Lactic acid 174

Levitational 57

Light energy 50

Light quantum 103

Lightwater center 65

Lilly, Prof. John 172

Liver disease 212

Lourdes 64

Ludwig, Dr. Wolfgang 68

Lymphs 57

M

Magnesium 109, 115

Matter 13, 20

Meander movement 57

Menopausal discomfort 224

Metabolism 45, 154

Metal salts 114

Microwave 39

Miller, Stanley 148

Mineral water 71

Minerals 27, 47

Moods 45

Muscle pain 174

Muscle tension 178

N

Nervousness 221

Neurodermatitis 158, 192, 193

Nitrogen 72

Nutrition 19

O

Ocean, primal 45

Oral hygiene 228

Organism 108

Organometry 17

Original Himalayan Crystal Salt 121

Osmosis 45

Osteoporosis 213

Ozonation 73

P

Paracelsus 60

Pasteurization 38

Peloid 181

Peristaltic 154

Pesticides 67

Photosynthesis 70

PMS 224

Pollution 137

Polyphenols 114

Potassium 109

Preservatives 114

Principle order 31

Proteins 99

Proteins, animal 41

Psoriasis 158, 193

Pyramids 29

Q

Quartz crystal 78

R

Regulatory mechanisms 10, 33

Relaxation 172, 173, 183

Respiratory diseases 128, 201

Rheumatism 211

Rock salt 116

Rubbia, Dr. Carlos 20, 50

Runny nose 209

S

Salt deodorant 230

Salt shirt 176

Salt socks 177

Salt chamber 128

Schüssler salt therapy 100

Schüssler, Dr. Wilhelm 100

Schuhmann resonance frequency 59

Segmentary diagnosis 17, 131

Self healing forces 10, 35

Schauberger, Victor 59

Short wave radiation 39

Sinus flush 166

Sinus infection 218

Skin diseases 174, 190, 229

Skin resistance, measurements of 17

Sleeping disorders 221

Sodium 146

Sole application 175

Sole bath 168

Sole drinking therapy 163

Sole flush 165

Sole fog

Sole inhalation 164

Sole mud 181

Sole wraps 176

Spiral 15, 56

Sprain 176

Spring water 71, 82, 162

Stomach aches 217

Supplements 19, 40

T

Table salt 88, 109, 121

Tap water 74, 78

Tartar 228

Thigh wraps 206

Throat, sore 207

Trace elements 99

Tumor 17

V

Vegan 41

Vitality, loss of 227

Vitamin B12 41

Vitamins 41, 99

W

Warts 198

Water, anomaly 48

Water, boiling point 48

Water deficiency 47

Water, revitalization 76, 78

Wave length 22, 24

Wellness 229

Wieliczka 127

Women's health issues 224

Wrinkles 229